358

Successful Techniques
For
Higher Profits

Robert Rachlin

Successful Techniques
for Higher Profits

MARR PUBLICATIONS, P.O. Box 1421, New York, N.Y. 10101

LIBRARY OF CONGRESS
CATALOG CARD NO.: 80-85150
ISBN 0-938712-02-0

Rachlin, Robert
    Successful Techniques
    for Higher Profits

New York: MARR Publications

First printing

Dedicated to
my wife Roseann
and my children
Melinda and Amy

Preface

As businesses grow and economic conditions change, the use of certain practical skills still remains a key to managing a business. Like any other organization, a business is constantly in motion. Although this motion may not be apparent at times, the business is both changing internally and reflecting changes in external conditions.

This book is designed to meet the challenges of today's changing environment by providing the practical techniques needed to manage a business effectively. For example, chapters 3 and 5 on managing cash deal with both measuring and effectively using cash and working capital. Discussion centers on identifying cash needs as well as analyzing and rectifying declining working capital.

Liquidity in general is discussed, as well as how to maintain adequate liquidity balances, the impact of inflation on liquidity, and possible solutions to improving liquidity. Other ways of managing your assets will also be discussed.

Chapters 6 and 7 focus on how to use capital investments profitably and provide the reader with evaluation techniques. Several useful checklists are provided for use as tools in operating within the capital investment process.

Chapters 8, 9 and 10 deal with understanding the nature of costs within a company. Such areas as understanding the types of costs, identifying a cost problem, and effectively using break-even calculations and the margin rate are explored in an effort to assist readers in understanding how costs behave within an organization and what remedies are available for coping with rising costs.

Other chapters deal with how to establish the right price for a product; how to develop effective budgeting, reporting, and control systems; how to develop a practical business plan; and how to determine a company's best method of financing.

This book will help you to develop the skills necessary for coping with high inflation and rising costs. It provides practical techniques to use in managing most business environments, and helps to maintain the managerial skills that are necessary to manage a business effectively.

As in previous books, I have presented a practical guide for the business community. All functional activities of a company will benefit from this book, and any individual who is responsible for or concerned about increasing profits should read it.

Contents

1

Analyzing Your Business
Using Ratio Analysis

Although much has been written about financial ratios, many business persons still do not understand the importance of ratio analysis as a business barometer in spotting trends. Ratios will not provide all the answers, but they certainly make it possible for a company to compare its performance to that of competitors, to industry standards, and between like periods internally. These relationships are important in that they highlight where the company was, where it is now, and areas that need attention, whether it be to remedy a deficiency or to make the business even better. Ratio analysis will provide the tools needed to answer the many questions that can arise in interpreting financial statements.

Understanding Financial Statements

Most businesses prepare two types of financial statements that provide the manager with a picture of how the business is performing. One type, the earnings statement, shows how much profit was made during a given period. This is done by recording all income received from selling the goods and by deducting all of the costs of manufacturing, selling, administering, and other activities in support of selling the product. The result is either a profit, in which case revenues exceed expenses, or a loss, in which case expenses exceed revenues. This statement is prepared each month and includes both revenues and expenses accumulated during a 12-month period to show profits or losses for a calendar year (January–December) or a fiscal year (any other 12-month period). It is an interim statement that eventually becomes part of the balance sheet.

The other financial statement, the balance sheet, gives a running account of a business. Because assets must equal liabilities plus shareholders' equity, or because the left-hand side of the statement must equal the right-hand side, the statement is said to be "in balance"; thus the term *balance sheet*. Because the results of the earnings statement are transferred to the balance sheet, the latter is the financial picture of a company at any given time.

Analyzing the Balance Sheet

The balance sheet is made up of two major components, namely, assets and liabilities. Assets represent what the company owns, and liabilities what it owes. Because the shareholders' equity is money belonging to the owners, it is considered a liability and is entered as such on the balance sheet. Subcomponents of the two major components are as follows:

Assets	Liabilities
Current assets	Current liabilities
Fixed assets	Debt due after one year
Other assets	Shareholders' equity

These subcomponents need further explanation, since they will be analyzed as part of the ratio analysis.

Current Assets

These are assets that are used in the normal course of business and that can be converted into cash more quickly than can other assets. They include the following:

- *Cash in banks.* As the name implies, money on hand or that held in banking accounts.
- *Marketable securities.* Temporary investments of excess cash in securities that are held for short periods.
- *Accounts receivable.* Monies sold on account and not yet collected.
- *Inventories.* Merchandise in the form of raw materials, in-process merchandise, or finished goods.
- *Prepaid expense.* Prepayments of items, such as insurance premiums.

Fixed Assets

These are assets that are not intended for sale but that are used in the manufacturing, distributing, warehousing, shipping, or selling of the product. They include such assets as property, plant, and equipment.

Other Assets

These are such assets as intangibles (patents, goodwill, trademarks) and deferred charges in which benefits are to be received in years to come.

Current Liabilities

As the name implies, these are debts that fall due within the current calendar or fiscal year. They include the following:

- *Accounts payable.* Monies owed creditors from whom merchandise was bought on account.
- *Debt due within one year.* Monies due lenders that are payable within the current calendar or fiscal year.
- *Accrued expenses.* Monies that are due, but unpaid, at the date of the balance sheet, including salaries and wages to employees, pensions, and insurance premiums.

- *Taxes payable.* These are the same as accrued expenses but are shown separately because of the importance of the liability.

Debt Due After One Year

As the name implies, these are monies owed lenders beyond one year of the date of the balance sheet.

Shareholders' Equity

This subcomponent represents the amount of equity interest that shareholders have in the company. Even though one owner may own all the stock, this equity still represents a liability on the part of the company to the owner. Included in this category are the following:

- *Capital stock.* The shares the owners have in the interest of the company. Such stock is either common or preferred.
- *Capital surplus.* An amount paid in by the shareholders over and above the par or legal value of each share of stock.
- *Earnings retained in business.* The amount accumulated and left in the business after payment of dividends to shareholders.

Analyzing the Earnings Statement

The earnings statement reflects the results of operating the business in a given period and may indicate how well it will do in future periods. The major components of this statement are net sales, operating expenses, operating profit, other income (expense), and net earnings.

Net Sales

These are revenues received from customers in exchange for goods sold or services rendered. They represent the prime source of revenues for the company and are affected by volume and price changes.

Operating Expenses

These are expenses associated with the running of the business in support of selling a product. They include the following:

- *Cost of sales.* Includes costs of manufacturing a product, such as materials, labor, and overhead.
- *Depreciation.* Periodic write-offs of expenses to account for the wear and tear of physical assets such as buildings, machinery, and equipment.
- *Selling, administrative, and general expenses.* These are expenses incurred in selling a product and other administrative and overhead costs of the company.

Operating Profit

This component is the result of subtracting the cost of sales and other operating expenses from net sales.

Other Income (Expense)

This component represents additional revenues received from income-producing sources, such as investments in securities, or additional expenses, such as interest expense on borrowed funds.

Net Earnings

Net earnings are the result of net sales less all operating expenses, net of other income (expense) and income taxes.

Now that the two types of financial statements have been defined, a series of ratios will be used to analyze them. It is important to remember that, by themselves, these ratios do not have meaning. They must be compared to historical data, other internal operations, competitors' performance, industry standards, and so forth.

Categories of Ratios

To make ratio analysis more manageable, ratios can be grouped into three categories. These categories highlight trends at different levels of the organization, much like an organizational chart. Each category focuses on a different responsibility level within the organization and relates to different parts of the business, as follows:

- *Performance ratios.* These follow the trend of the overall performance of the company. Because these ratios are viewed by the outside community as a way of measuring both current and potential performance, they are important to the overall success of the company.

- *Managing ratios.* These assist in evaluating the various components of the balance sheet and are used in managing such major areas of the company as cash, receivables, inventories, and debt relationships.

- *Profitability ratios.* These evaluate components of the earnings statement and effectively show how well a manager is performing, given his or her level of responsibility.

To compute these ratios, we will use the data given in the financial statements shown in Tables 1-1 and 1-2.

TABLE 1-1. The Profit Company, Inc.
Earnings Statement
19X2

Net sales	$700,000
Cost of sales	525,000
Gross margin	175,000
Other operating expenses	
Depreciation	5,000
Selling expenses	30,000

TABLE 1-1 (Continued)

Administrative expenses	$ 25,000
General expenses	15,000
Operating profit	100,000
Other (income) expense	2,000
Income before income taxes	98,000
Income taxes	48,000
Net earnings	$ 50,000
Percentage of net sales	7.1%

TABLE 1-2. The Profit Company, Inc.
Balance Sheet
19X2

Assets

Current assets

Cash in banks	$ 5,000
Marketable securities	7,000
Accounts receivable—net	80,000
Inventories	40,000
Prepaid expense	5,500
Total current assets	137,500
Fixed assets—net	18,000
Other assets	4,500
Total assets	$160,000

Liabilities

Current liabilities

Accounts payable	$ 38,000
Debt due within one year	4,500
Accrued expenses	10,000
Taxes payable	12,500
Total current liabilities	65,000
Debt due after one year	24,000
Total liabilities	$ 89,000

TABLE 1-2 (Continued)

Shareholders' Equity	
Capital stock	$ 40,000
Capital surplus	10,000
Earnings retained in business	21,000
Total shareholders' equity	$ 71,000
Total liabilities and shareholders' equity	$160,000

Performance Ratios

Net earnings to shareholders' equity measures the return that is generated from the owners' equity in the business when considering all risks. This ratio is important because it serves as a barometer with which shareholders can measure future growth and, ultimately, provide additional capital in the form of buying a piece of the equity, such as shares. The greater the ratio, the more attractive the stock to outside investors.

$$\frac{\text{Net earnings}}{\text{Shareholders' equity}} = \frac{\$50,000}{\$71,000} = 70.4\%$$

Net sales to shareholders' equity measures the amount of sales volume that is supported by the equity of the company. A proper balance must exist, and this balance will be reflected over a period of time. A high ratio could mean heavier than usual debt to support high levels of sales, whereas a low ratio could mean an underutilization of the company's resources or insufficient sales to cover the business activity.

$$\frac{\text{Net sales}}{\text{Shareholders' equity}} = \frac{\$700,000}{\$\ 71,000} = 9.86 \text{ times}$$

Net earnings to total assets represents the return on funds invested in the company by both the owners and the creditors.

$$\frac{\text{Net earnings}}{\text{Total assets}} = \frac{\$\ 50,000}{\$160,000} = 31.3\%$$

Managing Ratios

The *current ratio* measures the ability of the company to meets its current obligations. The margin of safety provided for out of current assets to pay current debts and the adequacy of working capital are two major features of this ratio. However, the receivables and inventories must be carefully monitored to ensure that they are in keeping with acceptable levels of performance. Other ratios such as the collection period and inventory turnover ratios will aid in this analysis.

$$\frac{\text{Current assets}}{\text{Current liabilities}} = \frac{\$137,500}{\$\ 65,000} = 2.12\ \text{times}$$

The *acid test ratio* supplements the current ratio by measuring liquidity and the ability of the company to meet its current obligations. This ratio emphasizes those liquid assets that can be quickly converted into cash. These assets include cash in banks, marketable securities, and those accounts receivable (net) that represent quick assets.

$$\frac{\text{Quick assets}}{\text{Current liabilities}} = \frac{\$92,000}{\$65,000} = 1.42\ \text{times}$$

Current liabilities to shareholders' equity measures the share that creditors have against the company as compared to the shareholders.

$$\frac{\text{Current liabilities}}{\text{Shareholders' equity}} = \frac{\$65,000}{\$71,000} = 91.5\%$$

Debt to equity measures the amount by which a company is financed by long-term debt or borrowed capital and the extent to which a company is financed by permanent contributed capital (shareholders' equity).

$$\frac{\text{Debt due after one year}}{\text{Shareholders' equity}} = \frac{\$24,000}{\$71,000} = 33.8\%$$

This ratio is sometimes referred to as "2.96 to 1," which is the reciprocal of the given ratio; that is, for every dollar of long-term debt there is almost $3 of shareholders' equity.

Net sales to fixed assets (net) reveals how efficiently a business is able to use its investments in fixed assets.

$$\frac{\text{Net sales}}{\text{Fixed assets (net)}} = \frac{\$700,000}{\$\ 18,000} = 38.9 \text{ times}$$

Net sales to working capital measures the ability of working capital to support levels of sales volume. Working capital is explored in Chapter 5, which will reveal that an increase in sales volume requires an increase in working capital.

$$\frac{\text{Net sales}}{\text{Working capital}} = \frac{\$700,000}{\$\ 72,500} = 9.66 \text{ times}$$

Fixed assets (net) to shareholders' equity measures the amount of capital invested in nonliquid assets. High investments reduce monies for other investments, such as working capital. However, favorable investments in fixed assets will provide favorable future earnings and will result in greater funds being available to the company (see Chapter 7).

$$\frac{\text{Fixed assets (net)}}{\text{Shareholders' equity}} = \frac{\$18,000}{\$71,000} = 25.4\%$$

Days sales outstanding, referred to as the collection period ratio, indicates the average age of net customers' accounts receivable. It measures the efficiency of internal credit policies and potential bad debt write-offs. The greater the number of days sales outstanding, the greater the possibility of past due accounts. The calculation is made in two steps. Step one measures the average daily credit sales.

$$\frac{\text{Net sales}}{\substack{\text{Number of days in} \\ \text{a year}}} = \frac{\$700,000}{365} = \$1,917.81 \text{ average daily credit sales}$$

Step two computes the day's sales outstanding by dividing the average daily credit sales into accounts receivable (net).

$$\frac{\text{Accounts receivable (net)}}{\text{Average daily credit sales}} = \frac{\$\ 80,000}{\$1,917.81} = 41.7 \text{ day's sales outstanding}$$

Net sales to accounts receivable (net) measures the turn-over of accounts receivable during a year. Higher ratios indicate more rapid collections.

$$\frac{\text{Net sales}}{\text{Accounts receivable (net)}} = \frac{\$700,000}{\$\ 80,000} = 8.75 \text{ times}$$

Cost of sales to inventories is referred to as the inventory turnover ratio. The lower the ratio, the greater the possibility that the inventory is excessive and that it may contain some obsolete items.

$$\frac{\text{Cost of sales}}{\text{Inventories}} = \frac{\$525,000}{\$\ 40,000} = 13.1 \text{ times}$$

Days sales on hand indicates the average length in days in which inventory is held before it is sold. Two calculations must be made. The first calculation results in the average daily cost of sales.

$$\frac{\text{Cost of sales}}{\substack{\text{Number of days in} \\ \text{a year}}} = \frac{\$525,000}{365} = \$1,438.36 \text{ average daily cost of sales}$$

The second calculation measures the days sales on hand.

$$\frac{\text{Inventories}}{\substack{\text{Average daily cost} \\ \text{of sales}}} = \frac{\$\ 40,000}{\$1,438.36} = 27.8 \text{ day's sales on hand}$$

Profitability Ratios

Net earnings to net sales measures the profitability of every dollar of sales.

$$\frac{\text{Net earnings}}{\text{Net sales}} = \frac{\$\ 50,000}{\$700,000} = 7.1\%$$

Gross margin percent indicates the margin of sales over the cost of sales.

$$\frac{\text{Gross margin}}{\text{Net sales}} = \frac{\$175,000}{\$700,000} = 25.0\%$$

Selling expenses to net sales measures the cost of selling a product.

$$\frac{\text{Selling expenses}}{\text{Net sales}} = \frac{\$\ 30,000}{\$700,000} = 4.3\%$$

Summary

Ratios must be compared to other averages for similar lines of businesses as well as to industry averages. Because ratios indicate trends, it is important to analyze and explain major variances, whether they are high or low. This analysis will provide a manager with tools for spotting warning signs of problems that can be remedied. Ratios should be consistently reviewed over periods of time so that trend movements can be observed. One must remember, however, that ratios are only tools and are not clear-cut solutions to all financial problems.

2

Successful Techniques of
Return on Investment

The concept of return on investment (ROI) is vital to the success of any business operation. Its importance centers on the fact that managers' prime responsibility is to maintain the existence of the business through the investment of funds that are entrusted to them. They are responsible for selecting the most desirable alternatives of many possible resource investment alternatives. In many cases this selection is based on those investments that are expected to produce the greatest profit.

Objectives of a Business

There are two schools of thought with regard to the objectives of a business. Both are equally important, and both play a major role in the operation of a business. However, the theory that focuses on aspects of ROI is the more commonly accepted one. This theory will be discussed shortly. First, let us discuss another theory that is sometimes overlooked.

It has been said that the ultimate purpose of any business is to survive, that is, not to maximize profits, but to ensure that losses do not occur. Under this concept, profits take on a slightly different meaning—that is, in order to survive, a business must produce rewards over and above any risks that are taken. These rewards result in a profit, which is the result of a business being able to cover the risks taken in a business activity.

Another theory states that the primary objective of a business is to provide an adequate return to the owners. This theory follows more closely the concept of ROI. It cites three major ways of providing an adequate return to the owners:

- By utilizing the funds of the company to ensure maximization of long-term profits
- By maximizing other resources of the company to ensure that it obtains the highest possible return without assuming any excessive undue risks
- By allocating resources to produce the highest possible return on investment

This theory also states that increasing owners' wealth can be accomplished by simultaneously accomplishing the following two activities:

- Maximizing profits, which is accomplished by increasing sales, increasing margins, and decreasing operational expenses
- Minimizing investment, which is accomplished by increasing inventory turnover, decreasing receivables, and minimizing unprofitable investments in property, plant, and equipment

Although these activities seem fundamental, accomplishing them is not always possible. The internal and external environments are not always favorable. Most well-managed companies are continuously aiming to accomplish these two activities, but sometimes circumstances do not create the perfect environment. When both activities are accomplished, companies prosper and growth occurs. However, one must keep in mind that other factors such as cash flow, personnel, economic environment, market share, product quality, and usefulness of product also play a major role in the success or failure. From an ROI point of view, however, maximizing profits and minimizing investment are paramount.

Why Is ROI Important?

The concept of ROI assists management in maintaining the necessary growth for survival. It assists in highlighting historical performance and enables managers to use such data in projecting future performance. This use is easily seen in the evaluation of capital investments, where future cash flows are projected and used to evaluate expected ROI. In addition, future overall company financial objectives are established using historical data as a base. Because ROI is recognized as an acceptable measurement technique, its value is unquestioned.

It is also important because it provides management with an easy and understandable mathematical calculation. This calculation is used to enhance the decision-making process through better planning, by assisting in the evaluation of investment opportunities, by evaluating management performance, and by evaluating the overall position of the company in relation to the marketplace.

What Is ROI?

Return on investment is a management tool that measures both past performance and future investment decisions in a reasonably systematic manner. It rests on the assumption that the best alternative investment is one that maximizes profits.

The definition of ROI depends upon the investment base used. If equity is used as the denominator base, the definition is *return on equity*. If assets are used as the base, the definition is *return on assets*. The numerator is the profit expected from that investment, such as before taxes, after taxes, and so forth. Like the investment base, it can vary. The ratio for return on investment is earnings divided by investment.

What Does the ROI Concept Do?

The ROI concept is unique in that it creates an atmosphere that is healthy for any organization. It defines a specific problem within the company, such as production efficiency, growing obsolescence of plant and machinery, lack of new product introductions, or decreasing share of market. Identifying problems is the first step toward solving them.

Once the problem is identified, alternatives are presented, and weighed against each other. An action plan is developed to carry out the selected alternative, and the investment begins to materialize. Thus the ROI concept accomplishes many management tasks. Managers must be involved at all levels of the organization, since ROI results occur from participation of all disciplines at all levels. It must be kept in mind that ROI is the concern of everyone involved in the business.

Major Uses and Applications

That ROI is everyone's concern is evidenced by the various uses and applications of ROI within an organization. These uses and applications create total involvement throughout the company. Some employees are affected more than others. The major uses and applications of ROI with a brief explanation, are as follows:

- *External measurement.* External performance compared to internal performance. Also helpful when comparing the company's performance to industry standards.

- *Internal measurement.* Answers the question regarding how well the segments of the organization are performing in relation to planned objectives.

- *Improving asset utilization.* Shows how best to utilize the company's assets in order to maximize profits.

- *Capital expenditure evaluation.* Concepts such as payback, accounting methods, and discounted cash flow techniques are used to measure expected future returns on a proposed investment.

- *Establishing profit goals.* Used as a tool to set financial goals based on historical performance and future potential.

- *Management incentives.* Used as a means to reward management for meeting stated ROI objectives.

- *Product-line analysis.* Used to evaluate the impact of adding or eliminating product lines.

- *Make or buy decisions.* Used as a tool to evaluate whether to make or buy a product.

- *Lease or purchase decisions.* The evaluation of lease decisions versus purchase decisions.

- *Pricing.* Measures the impact of certain pricing decisions and also is used to establish pricing where certain ROI objectives are required.

- *Mergers, acquisitions, and divestments.* Used to measure the impact of the activity of mergers, acquisitions, and divestments.

These major uses and applications of ROI highlight the far-reaching effects that ROI has on the company. Most decisions have an impact in some way on ROI performance.

Cautions in Using ROI

Three major cautions must be recognized in using ROI so that it is used correctly. First, one must not rely totally on absolute numerical results, which can be misleading when used by themselves. Such results need to be supported by an understanding of how the calculations were made and of how they relate to other numerical data.

Second, the calculations of ROI must be consistent from one period to another, since incremental changes from period to period are more important than absolute values. The end results can vary by merely changing the method of calculation. Therefore, consistency in the use of historical data as well as in future forecasting must be adhered to.

Third, one must not ignore other methods of appraising performance. Although ROI is an important barometer of success, it is not the ultimate evaluation technique. Other measurement techniques such as share of market, percentage of sales changes, management attitudes, and meeting budgeted projections should be considered in order to evaluate fully the performance of an individual and/or segment of a company.

Understanding the Components of ROI

To understand ROI, it is important to grasp its components. The three components are net sales, earnings, and investment. They are derived from the two major financial statements, the consolidated statement of earnings and the consolidated balance sheet. These three components formulate the two major segments of ROI, namely, the profitability rate and the turnover rate. The profitability rate is computed by dividing earnings by net sales; the turnover rate is computed by dividing net sales by investment. Combining both segments results in

$$\frac{\text{Earnings}}{\text{Net sales}} \times \frac{\text{Net sales}}{\text{Investment}}$$

which can be reduced to the ratio of earnings divided by investment. This ratio is the basis for calculating ROI. Before one can appreciate the ratio, however, it is important to understand each segment, because each reacts differently, and different decisions will have to be made in order to increase either of the segments.

Turnover Rate

The *turnover rate,* or investment turnover, is an indicator of how capital-intensive a business is, or how many dollars in investment are needed to support dollars in revenues. At a given level of sales dollars, one will find a somewhat linear relationship to investment dollars. For example, if we look at total assets as a base, the reasoning behind this statement is as follows: To support sales, assets are needed. Sales result in either cash or accounts receivables. Inventories are needed to support sales levels. Plant, property, and equipment are needed to produce the product that ends up in inventory, and either cash or receivables are obtained when the product is sold. Other assets usually are insignificant. Sales dollars will usually follow a linear pattern, since such a pattern is needed to support the sales volume. Most companies within an industry will find this turnover rate consistent over a period of time. Certain industries have a high turnover rate because of the nature of the business. Once a company's acceptable level of turnover is found, every effort should be made to improve this rate or, at the very least, to maintain this level.

Figure 2-1 can be used for identifying each of the accounts composing the turnover rate. Each account should be charted by using comparisons, such as this year versus last year, actual versus budget, and one's company versus competitors. The turnover rate shown in the figure uses total assets as a base. When using other investment bases, the accounts would change.

Profitability Rate

The profitability rate, or earnings divided by sales, reveals how much of earnings is generated from each dollar of sales. It is probably the most critical relationship in the ROI calculation. It provides the financial base on which companies will support their future growth. When excessive

FIGURE 2-1. Turnover rate.

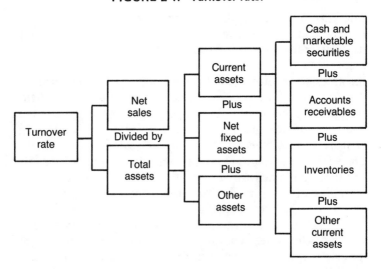

earnings result, they are put back into the business to support the future objectives of the company. Because use of internal funds is generally cheaper than external borrowing, it is extremely important that every effort be made to maximize sales dollars into higher earnings. Lack of earnings, and ultimately of cash flow, is one of the primary reasons why companies fail.

Another reason why the profitability rate is important is that it is the most sensitive to business decisions. In the short run, the profitability rate can be changed easily by merely reducing expenses. However, this is a short-run remedy and may jeopardize the company's existence if caution is not exercised. In addition, it is the one segment that can vary substantially in calculating ROI.

The profitability rate can also be calculated by product line, market, products, divisions, responsibility centers, profit centers, or any other business segment deemed necessary for proper control. Each of these segments should have a profitability rate objective, which must be measured against actual performance periodically. It is

FIGURE 2-2.   Profitability rate.

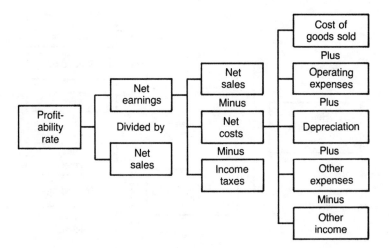

suggested that this evaluation be made no less than once a
month. Figure 2-2 shows how the profitability rate is displayed and how it can be analyzed at each separate
account level. Remember that, like each account in the
turnover rate, each account in the profitability rate can be
compared as to actual versus budget, this year versus last
year, one's company versus competitors, and so forth.
Note that different accounts can be displayed, depending upon the business and the needs of the company.

Return on Total Assets

When both the turnover rate and the profitability rate are
combined, an ROI rate is generated. Because total assets
have been used as an investment base here, the ROI rate
will be referred to as *return on total assets*. All the figures
are taken from the profitability rate and the turnover rate
and are displayed as in Figure 2-3.

FIGURE 2-3. Return on total assets.

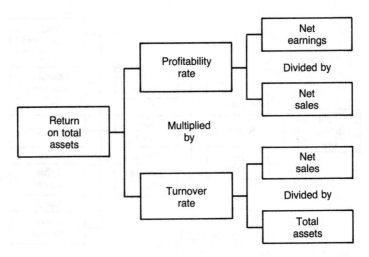

How to Increase Return on Total Assets

The ROI rate can be increased by taking a number of actions. Conversely, if these actions are not taken, a lower return rate will result. Briefly, the actions are as follows:

- *Increase sales volume.* Results in higher net sales, assuming that there are no price reductions.

- *Increase sales price.* Results in higher net sales, assuming that there is no loss in sales volume.

- *Reduce production costs.* Results in higher earnings, assuming that costs are not the result of lower production.

- *Reduce operating costs.* Results in higher earnings by keeping costs at a level to produce low break-even points.

- *Reduce cash balances.* Keep cash balances to minimal operating levels, and use excess cash to generate additional income. This results in lowering investment balances, increasing earnings, and, ultimately, higher ROI.

- *Reduce receivables.* Keep receivables to workable levels in relation to sales. Outstanding receivables should not exceed normal credit terms. Lower receivables will reduce investment, make available additional funds for operating the business, and increase ROI.

- *Reduce inventories.* Keep inventory turnover at acceptable levels. Enough inventory should be on hand to service customers, yet caution should be taken in watching for excessive inventory due to declining sales volume or product obsolescence.

- *Dispose of unprofitable facilities.* Constantly watch for facilities that are uneconomical. They should be disposed of or used for other purposes.

The ideal situation exists when all of the preceding activities are undertaken. Although they may seem basic, they are frequently overlooked and place considerable pressure on earnings and, ultimately, on ROI.

How to Analyze ROI

To determine which part of the ROI equation—that is, investment or earnings—is responsible for ROI variances, the two segments must be analyzed. By comparing actual performance versus budgeted performance, the variance can be explained. Let us use the following data as an illustration.

	Actual	Budget	Variance
Investment	$1,000,000	$800,000	$200,000
Earnings	$ 100,000	$120,000	$ 20,000
ROI rate	10%	15%	5%

What part of the 5% variance was due to investment, and what part to earnings?

Calculation

To calculate investment variance, budgeted earnings are divided by budgeted investment

$$\frac{\$120,000}{\$800,000} = 15\%$$

and budgeted earnings are divided by actual investment

$$\frac{\$\ 120,000}{\$1,000,000} = 12\%$$

The unfavorable investment variance was 3%.

To calculate earnings variance, budgeted earnings are divided by actual investment

$$\frac{\$\ 120,000}{\$1,000,000} = 12\%$$

and actual earnings are divided by actual investment

$$\frac{\$\ 100,000}{\$1,000,000} = 10\%$$

The unfavorable earnings variance was 2%.

The investment variance of 3% and the earnings variance of 2% composed the total ROI variance of 5%. These comparisons can also be made by periods, by competitors, this year versus last year, and so forth. This analysis answers the question of where the shortfall or increase took place and highlights potential actions that may be necessary.

Cost of Capital

One of the ways in which target rate objectives are established is by identifying the cost of capital to a company. This rate will identify the minimum rate at which an investment should be approved. It is recognized that other forms of establishing acceptable rates of return are available. For example, this rate can relate to the current experience of the company or to industry standards; can depend upon the risk factor; or can be tied in to the availability of capital, to past performance of the company, to government regulations in some cases, and to expected potential. Although all of these are important, it is most important to ensure that a company earns more than its cost of capital.

A typical definition of cost of capital is the average rate of earnings required to induce investors to provide all forms of long-term capital to the company. The definition itself highlights the importance of identifying an earnings rate that is higher than the cost of capital to a company. There are several techniques used to measure cost of capital. Two of these methods, the incremental cost method and the weighted average cost method, will be explored in some detail.

Incremental Cost Method

This method says that any investment whose earning rate is above the cost of financing is a favorable investment. Therefore, at any interest rate, an investment would be justified if one can earn more than the cost of that borrowed capital. To illustrate the point, let us assume the following:

Sales	$500,000
Earnings	$ 50,000
Total assets	$250,000
Loan of $50,000 for 5 years at 15%	

From these facts, one can see that the ability to generate earnings on new capital is 20%, which is calculated as follows:

$$\frac{\text{Earnings}}{\text{Sales}} \times \frac{\text{Sales}}{\text{Total assets}}$$

$$\frac{\$\,50,000}{\$500,000} \times \frac{\$500,000}{\$250,000}$$

$$10\% \quad \times \quad 2 \;=\; 20\%$$

Because the 20% represents the ability to generate earnings at that rate, it is now possible to compute the incremental earnings under the incremental cost method. To illustrate, we will use the preceding facts of a loan of $50,000 at 15% interest for 5 years, with equal installments of $10,000 each year. The results are shown in Table 2-1.

Table 2-1. Incremental Earnings

Year	Outstanding Balance	Earnings Potential	Interest at 15%	Incremental Earnings
1	$ 50,000	$10,000	$ 7,500	$2,500
2	40,000	8,000	6,000	2,000
3	30,000	6,000	4,500	1,500
4	20,000	4,000	3,000	1,000
5	10,000	2,000	1,500	500
Total	$150,000	$30,000	$22,500	$7,500

An easier way to compute the incremental earnings is to take the difference between the earnings potential rate (20%) and the interest rate (15%) and to multiply the difference (5%) by the total outstanding balance of $150,000.

The total of $7,500 incremental earnings means that, by using $50,000 of capital for 5 years, a return of 15% can be expected ($7,500 divided by $50,000). In addition, because the earnings potential is 20%, the cost of capital, as well as any acquisition of new capital, should not exceed this amount.

Weighted Average Cost Method

This method takes all the components of capital, assigns given values for each component in accordance with contractual and calculated rates, and develops a weighted average cost. These components of capital include both internal funds, such as retained earnings, and external funds, such as debt and preferred and common stock. Each of these components has a cost.

The cost referred to belongs to the stockholders, since they invest in a company with the expectation of receiving some future benefits. These benefits induce them to pay the price for the stock, in anticipation of future dividends and capital appreciation. In analyzing both benefits, one will see that they come from future earnings per share and are the principal factors affecting the price of the stock in the long run. Therefore, the stockholders cost is measured by the inverse of the price-earnings ratio, or the earnings-price ratio.

The price-earnings ratio is a reflection of investor confidence. Investors will react in different ways, depending upon their outlook. For example, when investors are optimistic about increasing future profits, they bid the price of the stock upward, thus raising the multiple. Conversely, when they are pessimistic about the future of earnings, or when they find more attractive alternatives, they tend to stay out of the market, and falling prices reduce the price-earnings ratio.

When reviewing the components of capital, one can identify the specific cost of most of the components, such as debt and preferred stock. However, the common equity presents a different problem and results in a different calculation. For example, it can be asked if earnings retained in the business have a cost. The answer is yes. This is so because stockholders view retained earnings as an opportunity cost—that is, when these earnings are retained in the business, they cannot be used to earn money elsewhere. In theory, the retention of these funds is the same as if dividends were used to buy the company's stock. Therefore, it is part of the money that the stockholder has invested in the ownership of the company.

The cost of common equity is calculated as

$$\frac{\text{Anticipated earnings}}{\text{Net price per share}}$$

or as

$$\frac{\text{Dividends per share}}{\text{Net price per share}} + \begin{array}{l}\text{Expected annual rate of}\\ \text{growth of dividends}\end{array}$$

The cost of equity is calculated to be 10%, given the following facts:

Anticipated earnings per share	$2
Net price per share	$20
Dividends per share	$1
Growth rate	5%

$$\frac{\$\ 2}{\$20} = 10\%$$

or

$$\frac{\$\ 1}{\$20} + 5\% = 10\%$$

The 10% cost of equity will be used in the overall calculation of the weighted cost of capital. Given the following facts, the weighted cost of capital is calculated to be 8%:

Long-term debt	$250,000 at 10.2%
Preferred stockholders' equity	$100,000 at 8.2%

Common stockholders' equity $350,000
Tax rate   50%

The results are shown in Table 2-2.

Table 2-2. Weighted Average Cost Method

Capital Structure	Aftertax Cost	Weight	Weighted Cost
Long-term debt	5.1%	35.7%	1.8%
Preferred stockholders' equity	8.2	14.3	1.2
Common stockholders' equity	10.0	50.0	5.0
Total		100.0%	8.0%

Note that the aftertax cost of long-term debt was 5.1%. Because interest costs are tax deductible, the tax rate of 50% must be applied to this cost. All other costs are already after taxes, and no adjustments are necessary. In addition, each of the capital structure components are weighted as a percentage of the total capital structure of $700,000. This weight is multiplied by the aftertax cost to obtain an average weighted cost.

The average weighted cost of capital—in this case, 8.0%—is used as a base for determining the minimum required cutoff rate of return on new investments. In other words, in looking at our previous example, management should not approve any new investments that are expected to yield less than 8%. Anything that yields less than 8% will yield losses, and any investment yielding more than 8% will yield profits. However, a sound management decision is to allow several percentage points over and above the average weighted cost of capital in case of errors in forecasting and unforeseen events. This decision will protect the investments' profitability in the long run. In this example, the minimum required cutoff rate would be 10%.

3

Forecasting and Measuring
Your Cash Needs

Every enterprise must provide the necessary cash for operating the business in both the short term and the long term. This cash is needed to ensure that the business will operate smoothly and that sufficient funds are available to meet both current and future obligations. Generally, short-term cash forecasts are for one year or less, whereas long-term forecasts are for more than one year. However, if a business requires shorter or longer periods, it is acceptable to change the time limits between long- and short-term forecasts. Let us explore some of the reasons for forecasting cash needs.

Reasons for Cash Forecasting

The following reasons should be used merely as guidelines for pointing out the importance of cash forecasting. Some of these points may not apply immediately if your company is new but will apply at some time during the company's life.

Expansion

In order to expand, large sums of cash must be available. The demands for cash in providing for expansion will play an important part in your future plans. In order to know how much and when cash is available, a cash forecast is necessary. Knowledge of advance monies will also assist you in making the best deal for additional funds, such as the equity and long-term capital markets.

Control

A cash forecast will assist you in setting up centralized control mechanisms that will enable you to know the amounts of cash available in the system, how much additional cash will be needed and in what period, and when to expect both receipts and disbursements of cash.

Payments

A cash forecast will highlight anticipated payments of loans, including interest payments, bonuses, major creditors, and dividends. It will highlight when these payments are to be made and whether sufficient funds are available. Having this knowledge on hand can provide you with the tool for shifting funds on a temporary basis to meet the demands of current payments. By using this technique, temporary shortages of cash may be avoided.

Investments

A cash forecast will point out how much and in what period cash will be in excess, in other words, how much and when excess cash can be invested in short-term securities. These short-term securities will generally yield high short-term interest, which is used to generate additional income. This becomes part of your cash management program.

Borrowings

From time to time, shortages of cash will result, especially in working capital. Seasonality may create a cash shortage that is temporary. Therefore, money may need to be borrowed to temporarily meet cash requirements caused by buildups of working capital such as receivables and inventories. The irregularity of flows of cash may require these temporary borrowings and is the nature of any operating business.

Requirements from Lending Institutions

Lending institutions will require that you prepare a cash forecast in support of any loan application. This enables the lending institution to determine your needs as well as your capability to pay back the loan.

A cash forecast is as vital to the operations of a business as are the financial statements.

Cash Forecasting Techniques

There are two generally accepted approaches to cash forecasting. One method deals with estimating cash receipts and disbursements, and the other method is a source and application approach. Let us review the cash receipts and disbursements method first.

Cash Receipts and Disbursements Method

This method is used for short periods of time, such as days, weeks, months, and quarters. It allows a company to forecast its cash inflows and outflows, or cash receipts and cash disbursements, in periods that are closer to reality. The basic problem with this method lies in its estimating of cash inflows or receipts. Errors in estimating receipts will invalidate any of the projections, particularly, as will be seen, the projecting of any short-term loan requirements.

In cases where a company has no historical base, it must use the best educated guess available. However, there are

Table 3-1. Collection Pattern of Sales

	Estimated Collections from Sales				
Month	Current Month	1 Mo. Ago	2 Mos. Ago	3 Mos. Ago	Beyond 3 Mos.
January	6 %	67 %	20 %	4 %	3 %
February	5	70	19	3	3
March	7	70	16	5	2
April	4	75	18	2	1
May	5	69	21	4	1
June	3	68	22	5	2
July	8	61	20	7	4
August	7	69	16	6	2
September	5	72	15	5	3
October	3	74	14	7	2
November	4	70	19	6	1
December	6	67	18	5	4
Monthly average	5.3%	69.3%	18.2%	4.9%	2.3%

sources where data may be obtained that would be of value in the estimation process. For example, market consultants, federal government statistics, trade organizations, local chambers of commerce, local colleges or universities, libraries, and local governmental agencies can provide data to help you in estimating the potential market and, ultimately, what receipts you can expect during the length of your forecast.

For companies with historical data, a simple analysis, as shown in Table 3-1, will provide some basis for cash to be received, assuming that sales forecasts are somewhat accurate.

One can see that applying the percentage for each month times the total sales will give you an estimate of collections for up to 3 months. Because the percentage beyond 3 months is relatively small, it is fairly safe to apply the percentage over the 3-month period individually. Using the monthly average as a base will provide an overall average, but the percentages for individual months are preferred.

Once the cash received from collections has been estimated, the amount should be posted on the cash budget form shown in Table 3-2. You should also estimate how much money was received from cash sales or from selling any assets and any other income that was received, completing the appropriate lines on the cash budget form.

The next step is to estimate the cash disbursements anticipated during the period. A realistic estimate should be made for each period. Many of these cash disbursements will be consistently the same. Caution should be taken to check the accuracy of each disbursement periodically and to reflect any changes that might occur in each forecast.

One must then calculate cash receipts minus cash disbursements. If receipts exceed disbursements, thus resulting in a positive figure, the company can expect enough funds to keep operations running smoothly. However, if disbursements exceed receipts, thus resulting in a negative figure, then a shortage of cash may result, unless the beginning cash balance is sufficient to cover the excess of disbursements over receipts. In any case, there is a cash drain on the business, and consideration must be given to remedying the situation.

Add the difference of net cash receipts over cash disbursements, and then either add excess cash receipts to the cash balance at the beginning of the month or subtract excess cash disbursements from the cash balance at the beginning of the month to obtain an ending cash balance at the end of the month. Remember that the ending cash balance becomes the beginning balance for the next month.

Estimate your desired working capital balance to operate the business and subtract from the cash balance at the end of the month. If the desired working capital balance is higher than the cash balance at the end of the month, then a loan is necessary to keep from being in a negative cash

Table 3-2. Cash Budget Form

The Profit Company, Inc.
Cash Budget Form
Period _____

	Period			
	___	___	___	___

Cash Receipts
Cash sales
Cash received from collections
Sale(s) of assets
Other income (List below.)

Total cash receipts

Cash Disbursements
Raw materials
Payroll costs
Other factory expenses
Tax payments
Purchases of machinery
Utilities
Office supplies
Rent
Insurance premiums
Mortgage payments
Other administrative costs
Selling expenses
Advertising
Loan repayments
Pension contributions
Shipping
Other (List below.)

Total cash disbursements

Net of cash receipts over cash
    disbursements
Cash balance at beginning of month
Cash balance at end of month
Desired working capital balance
Required short-term loans
Available cash on hand

---

position. These loan payments become a cash disbursement in later periods. However, if the cash balance at the end of the month exceeds the desired working capital, additional cash is available for such expenditures as capital expenditures, investments, dividends, and other areas where cash is needed for expansion. Additional surplus cash should be invested in an effort to generate a higher return than would ordinarily be expected.

Adjusted Net Income Method

This method is similar to the source and application of funds statement. It is designed to reflect changes in the company's balance sheet, with particular attention given to working capital. Like the cash receipts and disbursements method, it enables a company to see how items of the balance sheet will affect the cash balance at some future date and to determine whether it can generate enough funds internally or whether it must borrow funds from other sources and, if so, how much. Therefore, this statement measures the changes in accounts during a specified period that is usually longer than the period used for the cash receipts and disbursements method. The results reflect a complete analysis of both cash inflows and cash outflows. It will include not only working capital changes but also changes in nonworking capital accounts.

Source and Application of Funds Equation

In a previous chapter, it was pointed out that working capital represents the working funds of a company and is computed by subtracting current liabilities from current assets. Using the hypothetical Profit Company, Inc.'s balance sheet for year 19X2 (Table 1-2, page 7), the calculation results as follows:

$137,500 − $65,000 = $72,500

The difference of $72,500 represents the working capital of the company at that point.

In preparing the balance sheet, it must always be in balance. Total assets must equal total liabilities and shareholders' equity. Or, a more refinement of balance sheet categories states that

Current assets + fixed assets + other noncurrent assets = current liabilities + long-term liabilities + shareholders' equity

Applying the same figures, we get the following results:

$137,500 + $18,000 + $4,500 = $65,000
+ $24,000 + $71,000
$160,000 = $160,000

These results are said to be in balance. However, let us rearrange the equation to keep working capital segregated from the other parts of the balance sheet. By doing this we now have the following:

Current assets − current liabilities = long-term liabilities + shareholders' equity − fixed assets − other noncurrent assets

or

$137,500 − $65,000 = $24,000 + $71,000
− $18,000 − $4,500
$72,500 = $72,500

The left-hand side of the equation represents working capital, and therefore the right-hand side of the equation must also equal working capital. Sources and applications of funds can be computed by reflecting changes in either side of the equation. For example, if long-term liabilities increase and fixed assets decrease, this would represent a source of funds, since net working capital would increase. On the other hand, if long-term liabilities decrease and fixed assets increase, net working capital would decrease, representing an application of funds.

Source and Application of Funds Concept

The source and application of funds concept indicates how money flows through a business by highlighting where the cash was used and where it was spent. It will measure not only cash items but also noncash items such as depreciation. Although no cash is expended for depreciation, it is considered a source of cash in that it frees up funds through savings of cash on tax payments.

Computing the source and application of funds is relatively simple. By referring to the balance sheet for two comparative periods, one applies the following principles:

- *Source of funds*
  Net earnings
  Noncash charges
  Decrease in assets
  Increase in liabilities
  Increase in shareholders' equity

- *Application of funds*
  Increase in assets
  Decrease in liabilities
  Decrease in shareholders' equity

Before we apply these principles, let us discuss some of the decisions that affect cash favorably or unfavorably and that bring to light the importance of monitoring and controlling a business.

Decisions That Increase Cash

As will be seen later, many decisions have an impact on the balance sheet and ultimately reflect changes in cash balances. The following decisions, though not necessarily in priority sequence, are representative of those can increase cash balances:

- Reduce accounts receivable.
- Sell old and obsolete inventory.
- Sell unproductive assets.
- Reduce deferred or prepaid expenses.
- Defer payments to creditors.
- Acquire capital, both short- and long-term.
- Increase earnings retained in the business.
- Allowance for depreciation and other noncash items.

Decisions That Decrease Cash

On the other side of business, there are those decisions that decrease cash balances. Although many of these actions occur in the normal course of business, there are decisions that prudent management can make to prevent certain decreases in cash balances. Decisions that decrease cash balances are as follows:

- Increase accounts receivable.
- Build up inventory.
- Acquire fixed assets and other investments.
- Increase deferred and prepaid expenses.
- Make tax and dividend payments.
- Make payments for other operational expenditures.
- Make payment for short- and long-term borrowings.
- Sustain losses in operations.

Compiling the Statement

Having established the basic principles in preparing the source and application of funds statement, and having reviewed decisions that increase and decrease cash balances, let us compute the statement by first showing the changes and their impact on the balance sheet in Table 3-3.

Table 3.3. The Profit Company, Inc.
Balance Sheet

	19X1	19X2	Increase (Decrease)	Source or Application
Assets				
Current assets				
Cash in banks	$ 6,000	$ 5,000	($ 1,000)	Source
Marketable securities	8,000	7,000	(1,000)	Source
Accounts receivable — net	70,000	80,000	10,000	Application
Inventories	35,000	40,000	5,000	Application
Prepaid expense	5,000	5,500	500	Application
Total current assets	124,000	137,500	13,500	
Fixed assets — net	20,000	18,000	(2,000)	Source
Other assets	6,000	4,500	(1,500)	Source
Total assets	$150,000	$160,000	$10,000	
Liabilities				
Current liabilities				
Accounts payable	$ 34,000	$ 38,000	$ 4,000	Source
Debt due within one year	5,000	4,500	(500)	Application
Accrued expenses	9,000	10,000	1,000	Source
Taxes payable	12,000	12,500	500	Source
Total current liabilities	60,000	65,000	5,000	
Debt due after one year	25,000	24,000	(1,000)	Application
Total liabilities	$ 85,000	$ 89,000	$ 4,000	
Shareholders' Equity				
Capital stock	$ 40,000	$ 40,000	—	—
Capital surplus	10,000	10,000	—	—
Earnings retained in business	15,000	21,000	6,000	Source
Total shareholders' equity	65,000	71,000	6,000	
Total liabilities and shareholders' equity	$150,000	$160,000	$10,000	

As can be seen in the table, both total assets and total liabilities and shareholders' equity increased $10,000 as a result of decisions made between 19X1 and 19X2. One can also see whether these changes are sources or applications by applying the principles previously presented. A source and application of funds statement, shown in Table 3-4, was prepared using the previous data.

Table 3-4. The Profit Company, Inc.
Source and Application of Funds Statement
19X2

	Source of Funds	Application of Funds
Net earnings	$ 6,000	
Depreciation expense	5,000	
Decrease in Assets		
Cash in banks	1,000	
Marketable securities	1,000	
Other assets	1,500	
Increase in Liabilities		
Accounts payable	4,000	
Accrued expenses	1,000	
Taxes payable	500	
Increase in Assets		
Accounts receivable — net		$10,000
Inventories		5,000
Prepaid expenses		500
Fixed assets — gross		3,000
Decrease in Liabilities		
Debt due within one year		500
Debt due after one year		1,000
Total	$20,000	$20,000

Another way of presenting this statement is to reflect beginning and ending cash balances using borrowings as a means of supplementing the required cash needed to

Table 3-5. The Profit Company, Inc.
Source and Application of Funds Forecast

	19X2	1st Qtr.	2nd Qtr.	3rd Qtr.	4th Qtr.	Total
Sources of Cash						
Net earnings	$ 6,000					
Depreciation expense	5,000					
Total cash generated	$11,000					
Uses of Cash						
Decrease in other assets	($ 1,500)					
Increase in accounts payable	(4,000)					
Increase in accrued expenses	(1,000)					
Taxes payable	(500)					
Increase in accounts receivable — net	10,000					
Increase in inventories	5,000					
Increase in prepaid expenses	500					
Increase in fixed assets — gross	3,000					
Decrease in short-term debt	500					
Decrease in long-term debt	1,000					
Total cash used	$13,000					
Excess (deficit) cash generated	(2,000)					
Cash and marketable securities — beginning balance	14,000					
Increase (decrease) in bank loans	—					
Cash and marketable securities — ending balance	$12,000					

operate the business. Under this method, forecasts would
be made for succeeding periods, and borrowings would be
done according to the needs at different periods. A format
for a projection of four quarters is presented in Table 3-5.

A reduction of $2,000 resulted in the accounts of cash
in banks and marketable securities between the years
19X1 and 19X2. Because the beginning balance of
$14,000 was sufficient to cover the reduction of $2,000,
no additional borrowings were made. However, such a
reduction must be carefully watched to ensure that this is
not a continuing trend. Every effort should be made to
maximize the use of every cash dollar. Whether it be in
working capital or in investments, maximizing one's return
is vital to survival.

Summary

Forecasting and measuring cash needs will provide the base
for a successful and prosperous business. Be sure that forecasts and measurements are done frequently and as
accurately as possible. Continuous use of these techniques
will add insight, will assist managers in spotting trends,
and, ultimately, will help in developing a financing plan
toward continued growth and success.

4

Managing Your Assets

As an executive of your business, you are responsible for managing not only your assets but also other aspects of the business. For example, matters dealing with sales, purchasing, financing, cash, employees, administration, and so forth, are all your responsibilities. In many companies, these responsibilities are delegated to other managers who have the expertise to manage a particular segment of the business effectively. However, an operating executive must be knowledgeable in all phases of the business.

Although many executives concentrate on other phases of the business, managing one's assets is an important element of successful management—one that is often neglected. Many business executives are too busy trying to manage the day-to-day activities necessary to keep the business growing, as well as trying to meet the many pressures associated with operating the business. For example, attention is usually focused on such activities as increasing sales volume; maintaining adequate expense levels, particularly, costs associated with production; bank relations; financing; personnel management; customer relations; and overall office management.

Given all these pressures, executives may not have the time to consider managing the assets, nor will they consider asset management of any importance when faced with day-to-day problems. This is not to say that an executive has not, at times, given some thought to individual assets or, in some cases, to all the assets. However, priorities of time and urgency will usually win over.

In fact, the only time substantial attention is given to managing assets is when a problem arises. In a business that is rapidly expanding, problems usually arise with regard to the assets of the company. This chapter will make one aware of the importance of managing the company's assets, will provide some possible solutions to problems, and, most important, will establish a mechanism of periodic reviews to identify deficiencies in assets before they occur.

Classification of Assets

Because *assets* are defined as something of value that one owns in the business, we can easily group the assets to be managed into three major classifications.

Current Assets

This group includes assets that are anticipated to be converted into cash within the current operating year. In addition to cash, it includes marketable securities, accounts receivable, and inventories. These are considered working assets, which are used to operate the business and usually are converted into revenues by either a direct sale or in support of the sales effort. For example, cash is used to pay for manufacturing or for buying inventory for sale. Inventory is needed to fulfill sales, which usually result in an accounts receivable when goods are purchased on account. Marketable securities represent a temporary investment of excess cash, which is used to generate short-term income on idle cash. Figure 4-1 shows this relationship.

FIGURE 4-1. Flow of working assets.

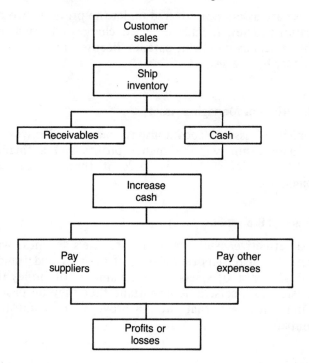

Fixed Assets

These are tangible assets that are not used for resale but that are used in the business to support it. They are also considered long-term assets, because they are usually used to operate the business beyond the one-year operating period. They include plants and related equipment, property, certain office equipment, and other physical assets needed in the business. Many of these assets will result in periodic charges or expenses to the earnings statement in the form of depreciation. In addition, a reserve is established against the fixed assets (except land) to ensure that recovery of the original investment is accomplished over the life of the asset.

Other Assets

These are assets not covered under the previous two classifications. They include deferred charges and such intangible assets as goodwill, patents, licenses, and investments in other businesses.

Objectives of Managing Assets

Managing assets accomplishes many objectives. The ultimate result will be higher profits and a financially healthy business. Let us look at three of the major objectives.

Method of Protection

With effective asset management, one's business will be protected against potential acts of thievery and fraud and against misuse of assets. With the amount of money that is invested in assets, it is important that they be protected against any act that would prove detrimental to the company.

Effective Use

Establishing sound asset management will highlight areas where assets are not being used efficiently. These inefficiencies can decrease profits in the immediate period or can begin to reflect problems that will arise in later periods. Each of the assets must be periodically reviewed to identify areas where wasted resources and excessive costs can be remedied.

Future Requirements

Effective asset management will highlight future asset requirements. These can be developed as part of the long-range planning process, which continuously highlights needs for future capital. Developing such a process will be a continuing task, as opposed to crisis decisions.

Although these objectives may seem basic, they must be formally approached as part of the evaluation process of the company. Like other areas of the company that are evaluated, assets must be properly evaluated if the company is to prosper.

Maintaining Liquidity

As will be seen in the next chapter, effective use of capital funds is enhanced by maintaining a sufficient level of liquidity. *Liquidity* means that assets are capable of being converted into cash in a relatively short period. Certain assets are more liquid than others, as evidenced by certain liquidity ratios.

For example, when a sale is made, an account receivable is established, whereby money owed the company by a customer will not be collected for several months. Tight control of accounts receivable will keep the liquidity of these accounts within the company's historical pattern and/or within industry standards.

In the case of inventories, an even longer period is required for converting the inventory value into cash. Because inventory must be either manufactured or bought in advance of a sale, one will not convert the inventory for the length of the accounts receivable plus the period between paying for the inventory and the sale. This situation is illustrated in Figure 4-2.

The figure shows that inventory was available for sale in period zero. It remained in inventory until it was finally sold 50 days later. When the inventory was sold, an accounts receivable was established, and the customer paid 35 days later. This means that the time between the acquisition of inventory and the company's recovering the investment of its inventory was 85 days. However, because the company did not pay the supplier for 25 days, the

**FIGURE 4-2. Illustration of the time lapse from
inventory to collection.**

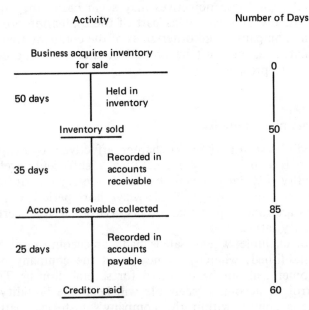

Activity		Number of Days

Business acquires inventory
for sale 0

50 days — Held in inventory

Inventory sold 50

35 days — Recorded in accounts receivable

Accounts receivable collected 85

25 days — Recorded in accounts payable

Creditor paid 60

actual time from when cash was paid out for the inventory
until it was recovered amounted to 60 days.

It is also obvious that for a period of 60 days this
money was tied up in both inventories and receivables and
could not be used for investment purposes elsewhere in the
company. If the inventory investment had been recovered
sooner, this money could have been used for other opportunities to generate profits. At the current rate of interest,
or at the rate for which opportunities were available, this
could have amounted to substantial earnings, which have
been lost.

Therefore, it is critical to ensure that inventory turnover
and day's sales outstanding in receivables are not beyond
the normal amount for your business. Every effort should
be made to improve these relationships, to speed up
inventory turnover, and to reduce the number of day's
sales outstanding. Should these periods exceed the norm,
critical cash shortages will occur.

Impact of Inflation on Liquidity

With inflation rates holding at the double-digit level, it is even more important for a company to practice asset management. Pressures on the liquidity of a company will begin to affect each of the major assets. Let us explore each asset separately.

Cash

With high inflation, cash is eroded because it takes more cash to buy the same goods previously acquired. Caution should be taken in watching for dangerous levels of cash insufficiencies due to inflation.

Accounts Receivable

Two major events take place. First, accounts receivable are inflated because of higher prices charged for the company's goods, which were necessitated by higher costs. Second, as cash begins to erode, as previously discussed, customers will begin to slow down their payments of invoices because they are also affected by liquidity pressures. This increases the length of time in which the company can expect to receive payment for the sale made. To offset this, the company may, in turn, delay payment of its invoices to suppliers, and the cycle continues.

Inventories

Like other costs of the business, the costs of acquiring inventory are inflated. This is due to higher costs for materials, labor, and overhead and results in replacing inventories that were sold at a much higher price. Thus this aids in driving the selling price upward in order to maintain acceptable margins.

Fixed Assets

Inflation also affects a company's ability to finance fixed assets, because it affects profits that are used to finance future investments. With lower profits resulting, companies may be forced to rely more heavily on external funds, thus increasing a company's cost to acquire needed capital. Another major problem is that inflation results in higher fixed asset replacement costs than is allowed by depreciation charges. It therefore takes more money to replace fixed assets at book value than allowable depreciation can recover. The difference of allowable depreciation and inflated replacement costs has to be recovered from earnings retained in the business and/or through additional external financing.

As can be seen, the cycle continues and develops into a continuous downward spiral, unless a company can manage its assets more effectively. Whether it be during the current period or in anticipating future trends and needs, the challenge is ever present.

Possible Solutions to Improving Liquidity

Good management practices dictate that certain guidelines be used to improve liquidity. These practices should be part of the asset management process and should be reviewed periodically for changes in one's business environment. In some cases, 6-month or yearly reviews are necessary. Whatever the time period, develop your company's review process by giving consideration to the following areas.

Managing Cash

Cash flow must be maximized by establishing an effective cash management program. Your bank can be of assistance in developing the latest system that best fits your needs. For example, such cash management techniques as lockboxes, wire transfers, and zero balance accounts will provide you with the knowledge and ability to maximize your cash flow. In addition, they will assist you in making use of excess available funds to generate higher returns for the company.

Managing Accounts Receivable

As was seen previously, buildups in accounts receivable can be costly. In essence, overdue accounts receivable put you in the financing business without a charge for interest. Because you have paid for the inventory, you can recover your investment only when you collect from customers. The longer the customers delay paying the invoice, the longer they have use of these funds at virtually no cost. Therefore, a sound credit and collection program is necessary.

The first step is to review the company's credit policy regarding credit limits, payment terms, and so forth. Tighten up on excessive policies that may be somewhat liberal as compared to those of your competitors. Be sure that you send bills on a timely and frequent basis.

The next step is to have an aggressive collection and follow-up procedure. Under this procedure, accounts should be followed up based upon the terms of payment. In certain cases, you may want to consider deposits on account or progress payments. Establish a policy for charges on delinquent accounts. Be sure that any discounts and terms are in keeping with those of your competitors and that they are rational to you and to the customer.

Paying Bills

Prudent cash management dictates that you should conserve cash where possible. This is true when paying bills. However, keep in mind that this does not mean that you should jeopardize your relationships with suppliers or your credit rating. It means adhering to the following basic principles:

- Pay bills only when they become due.

- Take all discounts available to you, assuming that they make economic sense.

- Inquire about extended terms from your supplier.

Managing Inventory

Inventory is much more complicated than the other areas. For example, in managing inventory you must be concerned with what quantities of inventory to stock, when and how much to reorder, trends in the marketplace for your type of product, and so forth. You must look for ways of reducing inventory levels by such methods as interchangeable materials and parts, cheaper material substitutions that can be made without affecting quality, product design to reduce raw material requirements, and so forth. Most important, however, you must closely monitor your inventory at all times.

Other Areas

Other areas of the company where liquidity can be increased are payment of taxes, lease versus buy decisions, changing inventory evaluation methods, changing depreciation methods, and taking advantage of certain tax incentives such as the investment tax credit.

Achieving the Right Mix of Assets

Almost all businesses are limited to the amount of assets that is available within the company. This limitation is dictated by the nature of the business, its size, and the growth of the operation. For example, a manufacturing operation would need more fixed assets than a nonmanufacturing company. The bigger the business, the more assets are needed to support increasing sales in the way of inventories and receivables. In addition, both credit limitations and equity in the business will determine the amount of assets that can be available.

The key is to maximize existing assets to the fullest extent, thus creating favorable returns. These returns are then used either to expand the business or to seek other favorable opportunities.

The question arises as to what is the proper asset mix for a particular company. The answer will vary from company to company and from industry to industry. However, several key elements of achieving the right asset mix can be identified. They deal with a basic strategy for each of the four major assets, namely, cash, accounts receivable, inventory, and fixed assets.

Cash

It is essential that enough cash be available to meet the demands of the company. Payments for labor, raw materials, supplies, taxes, rent, utilities, and so forth, must be made. Sufficient cash must be available to meet these needs, and historical patterns and cash forecasting will provide you with targeted amounts (see Chapter 3).

Accounts Receivable

To support any business that deals in credit, certain amounts of accounts receivable must be available to meet credit sales. One must expect receivables to increase as sales volume increases, but not out of proportion to a particular business's acceptable levels.

Inventory

In any well-managed business, sufficient inventory must be available to meet the needs of the marketplace. Inventory levels are based on anticipated sales levels and lead times to replenish the inventory.

Fixed Assets

Maintain the right level of fixed assets to support the company's activity, both in the short and the long term. Maintaining the long-term level will be accomplished by financing economically and financially sound capital investments. (For further discussion, see Chapter 6.)

A simple illustration can be used to demonstrate what happens to the individual assets when certain decisions are made. Assume the following simple distribution of assets:

Balance Sheet

Cash	$ 220,000
Accounts receivable	154,000
Inventories	240,000
Fixed assets	380,000
Other	6,000
Total	$1,000,000

Assume that additional inventories and fixed assets were required, amounting to $220,000. This would erase the cash balance of the same amount and leave the business with no cash to meet its other obligations. A similar situation can be drawn whereby accounts receivable could increase $220,000 because of increasing sales, and the same zero balance of cash would arise. One can see that balancing assets is a full-time job. There are no easy solutions, just constant review of your operation and knowing the impact of decisions that you make.

For example, when certain assets are in excess of adequate levels, the money that was invested cannot be available for other investments, which may be necessary for expanding the business. In addition, buildups of certain assets may result in a loss of value to these assets. Examples would be obsolete inventories, uncollectible receivables, and unproductive plants and equipment. Failing to recognize these buildups may, in fact, be detrimental to the business in a very different way in the future.

On the other hand, lower than adequate levels of assets can result in lost business. Not having enough inventory on hand to meet customers' demands will result in customers' seeking other suppliers.

Summary

Managing assets effectively requires constant review and the establishment of workable control mechanisms for your company. Throughout this book, mention is made of analyzing relationships for monitoring the business. Whether the problem be inventory turnover, collection period, or assets per employee, corrective actions can be taken before it damages the company. As indicated in the beginning of this chapter, sufficient time must be spent on managing assets for a business to remain competitive and operationally sound.

5

Effective Use of Cash and Working Capital

For many companies cash is the key element in maintaining a successful business. Without it, a company cannot meet the required commitments to stay in business. Even though a business may be experiencing sales growth, the necessary cash may not be available to meet the needs of increasing sales volume.

Two Types of Cash

It is important to distinguish between the two types of cash used for a business. One type is cash used for capital needs. For example, most businesses need cash to support the business in the form of fixed assets, such as machinery, equipment, fixtures, tools, buildings, and land. This form of cash is converted on the balance sheet from cash to fixed assets. It is this investment of cash that will provide the future earnings and growth for the company.

The other type of cash represents funds for working capital and is used to support the activities involved in operating the company. Such activities include the support of expenditures for inventory, the financing of receivables, payments to suppliers, and all other activities necessary to operating the business. Discussion in this chapter will focus on working cash, or working capital.

Cash Cycle

The cash cycle represents the continuous flow of cash through the operations of the company, resulting in an increase or a decrease in the cash balance. The flow of cash develops a circular pattern as it flows through the business, as can be seen in Figure 5-1.

The figure shows in a very simple way how cash balances are increased and reduced. Cash is reduced by payments to suppliers for raw materials needed to produce the product, and then additional costs, labor and overhead, are necessary to turn the raw materials into a finished product. When the product is ready for sale, it becomes part of the inventory. When this inventory is sold, monies are either immediately collected or receivables are established and collected at a later date.

FIGURE 5-1. Flow of cash.

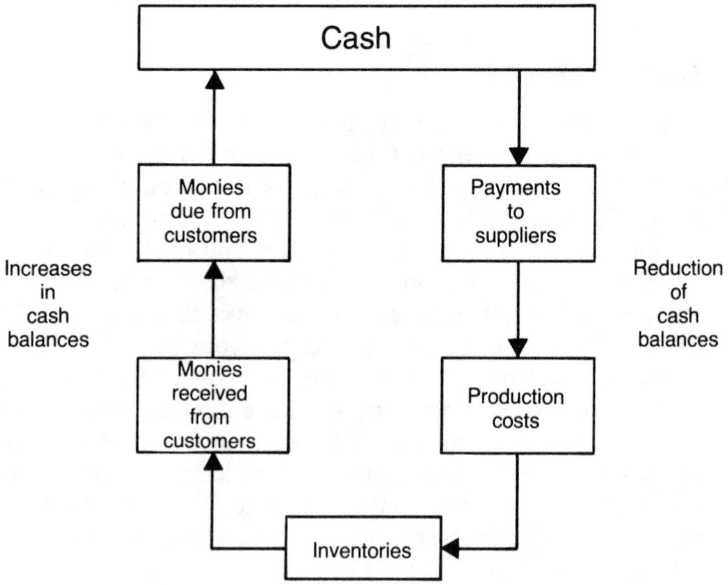

Although the cash cycle illustration appears simple, a problem arises in trying to coordinate cash inflows (increases in cash) with cash outflows (decreases in cash). The success or failure of a company hinges on its ability to monitor effectively both inflows and outflows of cash and not to be in a continuous desperate position for cash for any period of time. Such a position is both costly and ineffective, since an urgent need for cash does not allow the company to shop rationally for the best financing or even to generate those funds internally. In addition, it puts a strain on the operations of the company and stifles any growth plans.

Decisions That Affect Cash

Every business person is constantly faced with actions and decisions that lead to changes in the cash balances of the business. These are operating decisions that are necessary in the normal course of business. These decisions and some possible remedies are as follows:

- One way cash is generated is through the profits earned by the company. In order for profits to materialize, all costs of the company, particularly the margins, must be watched carefully. These margins, which are discussed in Chapter 12, are affected by the relationship among volume, cost, and price. High margins are the beginning of high profits.

- As will be seen in Chapter 13, reducing price to obtain higher volumes is not always a wise decision.

- Try not to purchase more raw materials or finished goods than are needed. Excessive inventory buying puts a drain on the cash balance, even though attractive prices may prevail at that time. Always anticipate what you are going to sell and plan production accordingly. This will dictate the amount of inventory needed to support the anticipated sales.

Remember that inventory unsold has a cost. Merely multiplying the current interest rate by the inventory value will give you some idea of how costly inventory is to a company. In addition, monies tied up in inventory takes away other profitable opportunities, which may have to be passed up because of cash shortages. Also, always take cash discounts when offered by your supplier.

- Avoid unnecessary expense commitments. This will keep your expenses under control and will assist in conserving cash. It is easier to avoid expense commitments than to cut expenses after the fact.

- Maintain reasonable credit terms. Accounts receivable that were generated from sales on account do not immediately add to your cash balance. Only when the receivable is paid does it add to the cash balance. Therefore, overdue accounts must be followed very carefully, and credit to customers must be screened. Remember that every dollar your customer has tied up in accounts receivable represents a loss of earnings (interest that can be generated) or a missed opportunity (such as capital investments). Excessive past due receivables are a danger signal to a company. This will be further discussed later in the chapter.

- Review periodically any fixed assets you own to potentially free up working capital. For example, some fixed assets may be candidates for disposal, and some may be candidates for sale and lease-back arrangements. In addition, look for fixed assets that are not being fully used. This opens the opportunity to consolidate facilities, move to smaller quarters, or rent to outsiders to generate rental income. All of these could be cash generators.

- Review periodically other parts of the company for the cutting back of costs, thereby conserving cash. Certain practices and policies in personnel, office supply purchasing, quality control, insurance premiums, production methods, scheduling techniques, security practices, and so forth, afford the opportunity for a company to conserve cash.

By conserving this cash, the assumption is made that it will be invested in a manner that will produce a greater return both in the short run and in the long run. If at any time you have doubts about the cost or about loss of additional earnings, compute the excessive cash tied up in such assets as accounts receivable, inventories, fixed assets, and even excess cash sitting in nonearning bank accounts. This calculation will certainly awaken you to reviewing your business somewhat differently.

Analysis of Working Capital

It has been seen how certain operating decisions affect cash balances. Most of these decisions are part of working capital (current assets less current liabilities). It is this working capital which is key to the survival of the company because it measures whether sufficient cash is available to meet debt obligations and other contingencies. The more classic definition is that working capital reflects the ability of a company to meet its current obligations, in other words, how many dollars of current assets are available to pay the creditors if liquidation were necessary or how liquid the company is.

To put this analysis into perspective, let us use a simple comparative balance sheet for 2 years, as shown in Table 5-1.

As explained previously, working capital is the difference between current assets and current liabilities. Between the years 19X1 and 19X2, working capital for the Profit Company increased $8,500, as shown in Table 5-2.

One can see how working capital increased $8,500 from 19X1 to 19X2. What does this mean? It means that the

Table 5-1. The Profit Company, Inc.
Balance Sheet

	19X1	19X2
Assets		
Current assets		
Cash in banks	$ 6,000	$ 5,000
Marketable securities	8,000	7,000
Accounts receivable — net	70,000	80,000
Inventories	35,000	40,000
Prepaid expenses	5,000	5,500
Total current assets	124,000	137,500
Fixed assets — net	20,000	18,000
Other assets	6,000	4,500
Total assets	$150,000	$160,000
Liabilities		
Current liabilities		
Accounts payable	$ 34,000	$ 38,000
Debt due within one year	5,000	4,500
Accrued expenses	9,000	10,000
Taxes payable	12,000	12,500
Total current liabilities	60,000	65,000
Debt due after one year	25,000	24,000
Total liabilities	$ 85,000	$ 89,000
Shareholders' Equity		
Capital stock	$ 40,000	$ 40,000
Capital surplus	10,000	10,000
Earnings retained in business	15,000	21,000
Total shareholders' equity	65,000	71,000
Total liabilities and shareholders' equity	$150,000	$160,000

Table 5-2. Changes in Working Capital

Changes in Current Assets

Cash in banks	($1,000)
Marketable securities	(1,000)
Accounts receivable — net	10,000
Inventories	5,000
Prepaid expenses	500
Total change	$13,500

Changes in Current Liabilities

Accounts payable	$ 4,000
Debt due within one year	(500)
Accrued expenses	1,000
Taxes payable	500
Total change	$ 5,000

Changes in Working Capital

Balance at beginning of year	$64,000
Add increases in current assets	13,500
	77,500
Deduct increases in current liabilities	(5,000)
Balance at end of year	$72,500

company is operating with more liquidity and that it should reflect some favorable ratio relationships, as will be seen shortly. However, it is important to be able to recognize and to remedy situations where working capital is on a downward trend. It is these situations in which actions must be taken in order to keep your company from experiencing a cash shortage.

Identifying and Rectifying Declining Working Capital

Declining working capital can result from deficiencies in many different areas of the company. It is generally an accumulation of deficiencies, or, in some cases, a major deficiency in one or two areas as receivables and inventories. Let us look at some of the areas in which declining working capital can occur and reflect on some possible solutions. Keep in mind that solutions can be different for certain companies at certain times of the company's maturity. However, most of these solutions apply to most companies.

Continued Earnings

Probably the most important factor for healthy working capital is to operate your company to obtain the maximum operating profit. Although this may seem basic, continued earnings will provide the internal capital for expanding and supporting the necessary investments in both fixed assets and working capital. Such comparisons as operating ratios, profitability ratios, and managing ratios will provide a barometer to flag declining earnings. Internal historical comparisons as well as industry averages are advised.

Collection of Accounts Receivable

Accounts receivable must be monitored periodically to ensure that the collection period is not lengthening. An aging of accounts receivable and comparison over a period of time will highlight deficiencies in the collection of funds. This should be an ongoing procedure and not a crash project when funds are low. Using the balance of $80,000 for the year 19X2, shown on the balance sheet in Table 5-1, a typical aging schedule would take the form that is shown in Table 5-3.

Table 5-3. Typical Aging Schedule

Name of Customer	Aging Schedule as of _____				
	Total	Current	31–60 Days	61–90 Days	Over 90 Days
ABC	$16,000		$16,000		
DEF	26,000	$26,000			
GHI	5,600			$5,600	
JKL	30,000	30,000			
MNO	2,400				$2,400
	$80,000	$56,000	$16,000	$5,600	$2,400
Percentage of Total	100%	70%	20%	7%	3%

Reviewing the aging schedule, with particular attention given to the "percentage of total" line, will indicate whether a downward trend is developing, particularly when compared on a month-to-month basis. Specific actions can be taken on specific accounts that show monies long overdue. It is important that you know your average collection period, so that a valid comparison can be made. Also, computing the ratio of accounts receivable to working capital will measure the impact of accounts receivable on the liquidity of your company. This will be explored later in the chapter.

Inventory Control

Caution should be taken in regard to investments in excessive inventory or in slow-moving products. It is important that inventory turnover measures be evaluated periodically to point out whether there may be buildups of excessive and/or obsolete merchandise. As will be seen later, this ratio (cost of sales divided by inventories) will highlight this deficiency when compared to previous historical data. Look for trends that may indicate a changing strategy in your business. An additional barometer is the measurement of the impact of inventories on liquidity by calculating the ratio of inventories to working capital.

Excessive Fixed Asset Investments

As explained previously, one way of investing cash is in fixed assets. However, caution must be taken not to over-invest in fixed assets out of proportion to investing in working capital. Although investments in fixed assets are important, cash must be available for the working capital requirements of the company. Careful estimates of working capital requirements will tell you how much money is available for other areas of the company, such as for fixed assets.

Cash Discounts

Taking allowable cash discounts offered by suppliers is a source of working capital. Review all invoices and schedule payments in accordance with credit terms, especially where cash discounts are allowed. Building up trade payables to conserve cash can not only result in loss of additional cash but also jeopardize relationships with your suppliers and ultimately lead to the company's becoming a poor credit risk. Cash discounts are a source of cash, so use them.

Summary

Look for problems that may be arising that could lead to declines in working capital. Watch your operations, bank balances, excessive expense commitments, loan payments, inventories, receivables, discounts, investments, and other areas in order to ensure that working capital is and remains a healthy ingredient in your business.

Working Capital Ratios

In any business environment, the true measurement of success is the comparative results of current performance to both industry standards and historical company data. When one says that "my current ratio is 2 to 1," it is only a general statement and does not mean much by itself. If the company's current ratio had been 3 to 1 historically, and if the industry's average is 2.8 to 1, then the current ratio of 2 to 1 is not very favorable. Therefore, it is important to have a comparative base from which to judge whether this ratio is favorable or unfavorable. Let us review some of the key working capital ratios, using the balance sheet previously presented. Additional data needed for calculations involving data from the earnings statement will also be presented.

The *current ratio* indicates the ability of a company to meet its current obligations.

19X1	19X2
$\dfrac{\text{Current assets}}{\text{Current liabilities}} = \dfrac{\$124{,}000}{\$60{,}000} = 2.1 \text{ times}$	$\dfrac{\$137{,}500}{\$65{,}000} = 2.1 \text{ times}$

The *quick ratio,* or *acid test,* is similar to the current ratio, but it places more emphasis on those liquid assets that can be easily converted into cash.

19X1	19X2
$\dfrac{\text{Cash in bank, marketable securities, and receivables}}{\text{Current liabilities}} = \dfrac{\$84{,}000}{\$60{,}000} = 1.4 \text{ times}$	$\dfrac{\$92{,}000}{\$65{,}000} = 1.4 \text{ times}$

The *liquidity ratio* is a refinement of the quick ratio, but it deals with the most liquid assets, cash and equivalent assets.

19X1	19X2
$\dfrac{\text{Cash in bank and marketable securities}}{\text{Current liabilities}} = \dfrac{\$14{,}000}{\$60{,}000} = .233 \text{ times}$	$\dfrac{\$12{,}000}{\$65{,}000} = .185 \text{ times}$

Inventories to working capital measures the impact of inventories on the liquidity of your company.

	19X1	19X2
$\dfrac{\text{Inventories}}{\text{Working capital}} =$	$\dfrac{\$35,000}{\$64,000} = 54.7\%$	$\dfrac{\$40,000}{\$72,500} = 55.2\%$

Accounts receivable (net) to working capital measures the impact of accounts receivable (net) on liquidity.

	19X1	19X2
$\dfrac{\text{Accounts receivable (net)}}{\text{Working capital}} =$	$\dfrac{\$70,000}{\$64,000} = 109.4\%$	$\dfrac{\$80,000}{\$72,500} = 110.3\%$

Net earnings to working capital measures the ability of your company to use working capital to generate net earnings.

	19X1	19X2
$\dfrac{\text{Net earnings}}{\text{Working capital}} =$	$\dfrac{\$33,000}{\$64,000} = 51.6\%$	$\dfrac{\$50,000}{\$72,500} = 69.0\%$

Net sales to accounts receivable (net) measures the turnover of receivables. Higher ratios indicate faster collections.

	19X1	19X2
$\dfrac{\text{Net sales}}{\text{Accounts receivable (net)}} =$	$\dfrac{\$500,000}{\$\ 70,000} = 7.1$ times	$\dfrac{\$700,000}{\$\ 80,000} = 8.8$ times

Cost of sales to inventories measures the turnover of inventory. Lower ratios are a warning that excessive and/ or obsolete merchandise may be present.

	19X1	19X2
$\dfrac{\text{Cost of sales}}{\text{Inventories}} =$	$\dfrac{\$375,000}{\$\ 35,000} = 10.7$ times	$\dfrac{\$525,000}{\$\ 40,000} = 13.1$ times

Net sales to working capital measures the turnover of working capital.

	19X1	19X2
$\dfrac{\text{Net sales}}{\text{Working capital}}$	$= \dfrac{\$500,000}{\$\ 64,000} = 7.8$ times	$\dfrac{\$700,000}{\$\ 72,500} = 9.7$ times

In summary, standards should be established and reviewed periodically so that, when working capital calculations are made, you will be able to recognize unfavorable trends and take corrective action.

6

How to Use Capital
Investments Profitably

The success of any company depends on investments that are made in assets. They provide one of the key elements of a company's growth in both the short term and the long term. Even in service companies, investments in people play a major role.

Types of Asset Investments

When one speaks about investments in assets, many different categories must be considered. However, such investments can be categorized into three major areas: physical assets, working capital, and research projects.

Physical assets are investments that are fixed assets, including such items as land, land improvements, factories, office buildings, warehouses, machinery, and equipment.

Working capital investments are those investments in the current working funds of the business that are used in operating the firm. Although it is recognized that current liabilities are part of working capital, only current assets will be used. Because current liabilities are a result of investing in current assets, one may consider them as another form of financing. Investments in working capital include cash, marketable securities, accounts receivable, materials and supplies, in-process inventories, and finished goods inventories.

Research projects are investments made for research in support of the operating functions of the company. These investments can be made prior to a major expenditure, such as a feasibility study of building a new plant, or expenditures can be made on an ongoing basis, such as for marketing research, production efficiencies, financial studies, and economic analysis.

Factors Involved in the Investment Decision

In any investment decision there are many questions that must be considered. These are questions that go into making up the final decision regarding "go" or "no go." Although the answers to different questions will have varying weights, all of these questions must be considered in the thought process preceding every project. Some of these questions may not apply to some projects, but a checklist should be made so as not to overlook any that may have an impact. A checklist is provided as a simple mechanism for ensuring that all of the factors have been considered.

To help you understand each of the complex variables, a brief explanation will be given for each variable, which will be phrased in the form of a question. Each investment will have its own characteristics and should be considered as a separate entity when evaluating the merits of the expenditure. Remember that each capital investment must be evaluated as if nothing else existed. The investment must be supported on its own merits.

What are the alternatives? Consideration must be given to reviewing alternatives to the proposed investment. The alternative may very well be to do nothing. If this is the case, one must ask the following question: What are the consequences over the short run and over the long run? Management should be presented with alternative options where feasible.

How important is the investment? Each investment opportunity must be classified as to its importance, both in terms of size and in terms of survival of the company. Investments that are very important receive a more critical review by more individuals. Investments of lesser importance usually require fewer reviews.

How risky is the investment? Every investment has some inherent risks. These should be noted by reviewing the potential consequences of not achieving desired results. It is the old "all-your-eggs-in-one-basket" theory. The degree of risk will also determine the level of return that you should expect. The higher the risk, the higher the expected return; the lower the risk, the lower the return.

What is the effect on the financial structure of the company? Many investments will change the financial structure of a company's balance sheet. This may be favorable or unfavorable in both the short and the long run. The impact on the balance sheet may create a negative situation for future financing negotiations.

Is this the right time for this investment? Throughout the history of business, timing of investments has played a major role in the success or failure of a product and, in some cases, of the company. Before approving any investment, determine whether the timing is right. This would include plant expansion, new products, expanding markets, new markets, increasing raw materials, inventory stockpiling, and so forth.

How will competitors react? Most companies will not enjoy the competitive edge for long periods. As soon as a company begins to flourish and to have a competitive advantage, competitors will react. Therefore, when investment decisions give you the competitive edge, be sure that you are not led to expect continued upward movement, particularly at the same rate of growth.

Does the investment have a desirable rate of return? In keeping with overall company objectives, does the investment assist in meeting these objectives? Will it enhance the rate of return in future years? Is it necessary to maintaining the existence of the business? Is the rate of return in keeping with the riskiness of the investment? How does it relate to competitive investment rates? Is it in keeping with industry averages? Does it exceed the company's cost of capital? These are some of the questions that must be answered to determine whether the rate of return is desirable.

How will the investment affect the financial results, both in the short run and in the long run? Because profits are derived from investments that have been made in the past and from those that will be made in the future, this question is critical. Many companies fail because poor investments were made, which did not produce sufficient profits to meet rising costs. Cash flow analysis will assist in validating estimated future profits. Its validity is only as good as the soundness of the projections. Knowing the impact of these investments in both the short and the long run will assist managers in planning future growth and future financial needs.

How reliable are the projections of the contents of the investment? The reliability of the investment data will depend upon such analyses as experience with other similar investments internally, engineering studies, feasibility studies, competitor experience with similar projects, and industry studies. Every effort should be made to validate the contents of each major investment, since the risk with larger investments is greater.

Does the investment deviate from the image and philosophy of the company? Every company projects some image to its customers and certainly has a basic philosophy in operating the business. It is important that investments reflect the image and philosophy since recognition by the marketplace may not occur, particularly when the introduction of new products is involved.

Does the investment meet the approval of all concerned? The investment should be approved by all responsible individuals involved in the business. Because each individual will have a different perspective, that is, a different background and different area of expertise, universal consensus should be strived for. This is even more important on major investments.

Table 6-1. Investment Checklist

	Very Favorable	Favorable	Unfavorable
What are the alternatives?			
How important is the investment?			
How risky is the investment?			
What is the effect on the financial structure of the company?			
Is this the right time for the investment?			
How will competitors react?			
Does the investment have a desirable rate of return?			
How will the investment effect the financial results, both in the short run and in the long run?			
How reliable are the projections of the contents of the investment?			
Does the investment deviate from the image and philosophy of the company?			
Does the investment meet the approval of all concerned?			
Are there any legal problems as a result of this investment?			
Are there any unique political situations involved?			

Are there any legal problems as a result of this invest-ment? Most investments should be cleared by legal counsel. Because many new laws affect many aspects of operating a business, it is important that significant invest-ments be reviewed by an attorney or legal counsel.

Are there any unique political situations involved? This is a hard question to answer, since many of these observa-tions are difficult to access. However, in certain circum-stances, local political situations may have more meaning. Major investments may be tied more closely with national policy, such as changes in the tax laws, conservation policies, or foreign policy.

Investment Checklist

For each investment, and particularly for capital invest-ments, check the appropriate box on the checklist shown in Table 6-1. That is, does the answer to a question indicate a very favorable, favorable, or unfavorable condi-tion? Where the question does not apply, indicate "N/A" for "not applicable." A glance at the checklist will show where there are problems with certain aspects of the investment. If there are areas showing unfavorable condi-tions, try to weigh the importance of these factors to the overall success of the investment. It is at this point that some decision should be reached. If there is still some doubt, further analysis should be done in an effort to clarify any doubts.

The Capital Investment Process

The process of generating capital investments within a company involves many steps. The actual mechanics of execution may vary, but the basic steps still apply. In essence, it is a problem-solving exercise, one that encom-passes the definition of a problem or opportunity and the implementation and completion of a project. A brief summary will be given of the total process.

Determining the Need for an Investment

This is the initial stage, which establishes the existence of a problem or an opportunity. This need will be generated at all levels of the company and at all locations. It may be in the form of adopting new technology, doing things better and in a less costly way, entering the marketplace with new ideas through new products, or merely making an investment for employee safety and morale.

Other Solutions

In conjunction with the first step, alternative solutions should be reviewed as a means of establishing procedures for evaluating which alternative should be chosen.

Determining the Availability of Funds

Total investments should be consolidated and coordinated with the total availability of funds for the company. If future funds are required, additional financing may be necessary. In addition, be sure that investments are in keeping with the long-range plans of the company.

Developing Measurement Tools

As part of the capital investment process, evaluation techniques must be established to measure and weigh the consequences of each alternative investment. These measurement tools are found in such techniques as payback, accounting rate of return, net present value, internal rate of return, risk analysis, and sensitivity analysis.

Developing Cash Flow Estimates

Each investment will have varying cash flow estimates. Cash flow represents all estimates of the project making up the net earnings, plus depreciation charges, additions to working capital, and fixed asset investment dollars. These projections will be estimated for each period (usually one year) over the life of the capital investment. "Life" in this case can represent either the physical life, the technological life, or the economic life. Whichever life is used, it will determine how many years' estimates of cash flow are necessary.

Establishing an Approval Process

Each investment must be reviewed as an individual entity and must support itself throughout the life of the project. Therefore, every investment must be approved by individuals assigned this responsibility. For example, each company must establish dollar limits at each authority level of the organization. At each such level, certain individuals would have certain dollar limits of approval; for a level over and above a stated amount, the board of directors would have to give final approval. These dollar amounts must be reviewed periodically in order to meet the growing demands of the company as well as rising costs.

Establishing Expenditure Controls

Once the investment has been approved, expenditure controls should be established to ensure that actual spending is in keeping with authorized expenditures. A mechanism for doing this is to resubmit a summary of the approved project with a request to issue funds for segments of the proposal against the authorized amounts. Amounts, vendors, purpose, and timing of expenditures should be included. In addition, a total of how much has been spent for the project and any underruns or overruns that are expected should be included.

Identifying Disposal Candidates

When a proposal is submitted, it should contain any candidates of fixed assets that can be disposed of during the life of the investment. Sometimes trade-ins as well as disposals are involved, helping to offset the initial investment cost. This helps in increasing cash flow, speeds up the payback period, and ultimately increases the return on investment.

Developing Forms and Procedures

This step will vary by company, but should include all the data necessary to make a valid and intelligent decision on the investment. The key is to standardize the forms and procedures so that all investments have an equal opportunity for approval. Standardization means using the same depreciation methods, the same method of calculating cash flow, the same calculation methods for payback and return on investment, and the same methods of presenting the data. Once this discipline is cohesive, an individual can fairly and more accurately measure the validity of what is presented. It also establishes an individual's self-discipline in making sure that all aspects of the proposal are considered.

Why is a Capital Program Necessary?

In order to reach planned growth, a formal capital program is necessary. It is necessary to ensuring that strategies, plans, objectives, and goals are met in an orderly fashion. Some of the reasons for operating with a formal capital program that is properly controlled and administered are as follows:

- Coordinates short-term programs with long-term goals
- Assists in utilizing the advantages of tax legislation
- Selects and determines those capital investments that offer the highest return and benefits to the company
- Determines the financial capabilities of meeting capital expenditure needs

- Identifies the type of equipment necessary to meet specific needs
- Determines the best method of financing
- Establishes authorization levels
- Determines accountability for acquired assets
- Highlights timing of investment with actual needs
- Indicates the timing of cash needs

Capital Investment Classifications

Most companies use different terminology for different types of capital projects. Although the terms may vary, they fall into the following general categories:

- *Expansion capacity.* Projects whose primary purpose is to increase production.

- *New product introduction.* Projects whose primary objective is providing facilities for the introduction of new products. New products in this case are those not currently manufactured and/or marketed by the company.

- *Cost reduction.* Projects that result in the reduction of costs.

- *Replacement and maintenance.* These are projects that are essential to maintaining the current status of the business. They do not increase capacity or reduce costs. Examples of such projects are quality improvements, health and safety requirements, quality control, testing, servicing, and the maintenance of the existing facilities.

- *Others.* These are projects that do not fall under any of the preceding classifications. Examples are contaminant control, employee morale, and certain office facilities.

Where projects provide for more than one benefit, it is necessary to determine which benefit is the primary objective of the project. This is done by reviewing the end results of the project and the major phase of the project creating the benefit.

Justification of Capital Expenditures

Each capital investment must be supported by complete documentation to justify the spending of those funds. As discussed previously, forms and procedures are required in order to standardize the presentation of capital investments. Each capital investment request should include both financial and economic justification. The financial justification should consist of a financial projection of the periods within the project's life, including working capital requirements, fixed asset investments, earnings projections, taxes, depreciation, cash flow generated, payback period, return on investment rate, and a justification analysis summary.

The economic justification should also accompany each capital investment request, further justifying approval of the investment. This addition to the proposal is simply a narrative documentation of the pertinent background and reasoning leading to the decision to seek approval for the project. Although the contents will vary from project to project, certain data will always be present. These include the title and identification number of the project; its classification (previously discussed); the purpose of the expenditure; why the present situation is inadequate, if it is; possible alternative solutions; financial justification; risk involved; projected market conditions; and recommended actions.

Calculation of Cash Flow

As indicated previously, calculation of cash flows is necessary to projecting the expected financial results of a specific investment. Projections are made over the life of the project and provide the basis for calculating cash flows and, ultimately, the return on investment. The following data are necessary for cash flow projections:

- Life of the asset
- Depreciation method
- Amount of investment
- Types of investments (machinery, equipment, etc.)
- Classification of investment (expansion, cost reduction, etc.)
- Working capital requirements
- Manpower changes
- Salvage and disposal values
- Earnings projections

With this information, cash flow projections can be calculated for each period over the life of the project.

Given the same simplified data for 3 years, the cash flow results from accounting net earnings plus depreciation charges are shown in Table 6-2. These data would be used

Table 6-2. Calculation of Cash Flow

	Year 1	Year 2	Year 3
Net sales	$5,000	$7,000	$10,000
Costs (excluding depreciation)	3,000	4,200	6,500
Depreciation	500	1,000	1,500
Earnings before tax	1,500	1,800	2,000
Taxes	750	900	1,000
Accounting net earnings	$ 750	$ 900	$ 1,000
Cash flow	$1,250	$1,900	$ 2,500

Table 6-3. Impact of Depreciation on Cash Flow

	A	B	Difference
Net sales	$10,000	$10,000	—
Costs (excluding depreciation)	6,500	6,500	—
Depreciation	—	1,500	$1,500
Earnings before tax	3,500	2,000	(1,500)
Taxes	1,750	1,000	(750)
Accounting net earnings	1,750	1,000	(750)
Plus depreciation	—	1,500	1,500
Cash flow	$ 1,750	$ 2,500	$ 750

to compute the necessary calculations for determining the payback period and the return on investment.

To further explain why depreciation is added back to net earnings and is used to calculate cash flow, let us look at the data for Year 3 as an example. Assume also that Example A in Table 6-3 has no charge for depreciation and that Example B is as given in the table.

The increase of $750 in cash flow represents the after-tax savings of depreciation. Although depreciation is not a source of cash, it provides higher cash flows by reducing income taxes paid.

Capital Expenditure Checklist

Some companies complete an extensive checklist of items to consider when preparing a capital expenditure request. Some of these items do not pertain to all projects; in many cases, they relate to projects in which new products are involved. Nevertheless, it is important to have such a checklist so that all areas of the project are at least considered. The checklist is broken down into the following segments:

- Financial
- Investment
- Distribution/warehousing
- Pricing
- Market
- Technical
- Production
- Labor
- Inventory

Some of the significant questions that must be answered or explored for each capital expenditure request will be given for each of the preceding segments. This checklist, which is given in Table 6-4, is by no means comprehensive and should be supplemented by other areas that are unique to a particular company.

Table 6.4. Capital Expenditure Checklist

Financial

What is the financial risk?

Can product investment generate sufficient cash flow?

What is the cash risk, or payout?

What is the expected rate of return?

Is there any internal or external transfer of profits? If so, how much?

What is the break-even point?

What financing will be required?

What are the tax implications?

How will overhead be allocated?

Investment

If this project is a replacement of existing machinery and equipment, what disposition will be made of the old machinery and equipment?

Table 6.4 (continued)

Distribution/Warehousing

If capacity is increased, what will be the impact on storing and distribution facilities?

Are any new distribution channels required?

Can the product be distributed by the current sales organization?

By what method will the product be distributed?

Pricing

Is the selling price dependent upon the production costs?

What is the elasticity of the price on supply and demand?

What pricing strategy has been planned?

At what price will the break-even point occur?

What is the expected price trend?

Market

What is the ease of entry by competitors if the product is new to the marketplace?

What is the nature of the market, that is, size, industry, and so forth?

At what state is the current market? That is, is it expanding, contracting, or maintaining position?

How do customers react to changes in the economy, in needs, and in trends?

Who are the major competitors?

How strong a position do the competitors have in the marketplace?

Are our proposed products competitive?

Are there any restrictions set forth by the marketplace or by governmental regulations that limit both production and sales?

Is this product for domestic consumption only?

What is the demand for potential business?

If the investment is product related, has the product been tested?

Are there any additional costs involved in promoting the product?

Technical

What are the risks in technically completing the project?

How likely are the chances of changes in technology or the risk of obsolescence?

Table 6.4 (continued)

If this is a new process, what are the potential problems?

Are there any additional requirements for maintenance?

What is the technical know-how of the proposed project?

Will new machinery and equipment require new design?

Does the project require new plant layout?

Will the start-up situation require additional resources?

Can technical service be provided to new customers for new products?

Are any patent problems involved?

Is specialized know-how needed to produce this product?

Are there any salable by-products as a result of this project?

Production

How will this project affect production rates?

Does the projected volume of production seem reasonable given the current rate?

How flexible are the planned facilities for future expansion?

Why are changes to current production facilities necessary?

What is the history of repair and maintenance costs if equipment and machinery are being replaced?

Can new facilities produce other related products?

Is the product seasonal, and if so, what is the impact on production levels?

Labor

Will the project require any additional labor?

Will the project reduce labor costs, and by how much?

Inventory

Are new sources of raw materials needed?

What are the required inventory levels?

How accessible are producers of raw material to production facilities?

Is there more than one supplier of raw materials?

7

How To Successfully Evaluate
Capital Investments

The success of most companies depends upon the maximum use of capital investments. Profits are generated through capital investments by providing additional earnings that are generated by a specific investment. Growth companies will continue to plow back earnings into profitable investments and in some cases will borrow funds to finance profitable opportunities.

This chapter will deal with the concepts involved in evaluating capital investments. Each of the many concepts has its advantages and disadvantages. Ultimately, the method that fits a company's needs is the one that should be used. The key is to establish consistency both in technique and in computation, so that each investment is evaluated against another. The next step is to select those investments that are necessary to the growth of the company.

The Prerequisites of an
Acceptable Method of Calculation

Certain prerequisites are important for the overall effective evaluation of capital investments. Each is part of the overall process, and its importance cannot be overemphasized. The prerequisites are as follows:

- *Universal application.* The method must be capable of being applied throughout the entire organization. Its universal application must be understood and workable for all parts of the organization.

- *Time value of money.* Because money has a cost and is related to time, it is important that a method of calculation include the time value of money. This is found when computing discounted cash flow, which will be discussed later.

- *Consideration of the life of the project.* The method must consider the life of the project, whether it be the economic, technological, or physical life. The total life must be considered in order to evaluate fully the effectiveness of the project.

- *Consideration of the payback period.* This is accomplished by using the payback method of evaluation. As will be discussed later, the payback method measures recoverability and not rate of return. Therefore, it is one of the calculations used in conjunction with other methods for evaluating capital investments.

- *Ease of calculation.* Because the preparers will be from different disciplines throughout the company, and because the expertise of these individuals may not be uniformly sophisticated, the calculation should be reasonably easy to carry out.

- *Consideration of the risk.* The method must be capable of highlighting certain elements of risk. Whether it be cash risk, financial risk, or obsolescence, it is important that it be reflected in a good method of calculation.

Calculation of Cash Flow

To evaluate the financial justification of capital investments, it is necessary to calculate the cash flow that is generated from a specific project. The cash flow projections are found in the capital expenditure request form and include the following financial information:

- *Investment*
  Land
  Buildings
  Machinery and equipment
  Working capital
  Capitalized costs
  Other

- *Earnings*
  Net sales
  Cost of sales
  Advertising
  Research
  Depreciation
  Selling
  General and administrative
  Taxes
  Other

Projections are made for each time period over the life of the investment, as are earnings projections. With this information, cash flows are calculated by taking the yearly projections over the life of the investment and applying the following formula: accounting net earnings plus depreciation charges.

Given the following data about a project,

Machinery and equipment	$80,000
Working capital	40,000
Depreciation method	Straight line
Life of asset	4 years

the cash flow statement shown in Table 7-1 results.

Table 7-1. Illustration of Cash Flow for a Project (In $1,000s)

	Year				
	0	1	2	3	4
Machinery and equipment	$ 80				
Working capital	40				
Total investment	$120				
Net sales		$120	$120	$120	$120
Costs (excluding depreciation)		60	60	60	60
Depreciation		20	20	20	20
Earnings before taxes		40	40	40	40
Taxes		20	20	20	20
Net earnings		$ 20	$ 20	$ 20	$ 20
Cash flow		$ 40	$ 40	$ 40	$ 40

The data in Table 7-1 will be used in the necessary calculations for determining the payback period and the return on investment.

To further explain why depreciation is added back to net earnings and is used to calculate cash flow, let us look at the preceding data for all 4 years of cash flow. Assume also that Example A in Table 7-2 has no charge for depreciation and that Example B is as given.

The increase of $40,000 in cash flow represents the aftertax savings of depreciation. Although depreciation is not a source of cash, it provides higher cash flows by reducing income taxes paid.

Payback

The payback method has long been used in capital expenditure evaluations. As will be seen, it is a method that

Table 7-2. Impact of Depreciation on Cash Flow (In $1,000s)

	A	B	Difference
Net sales	$480	$480	—
Costs (excluding depreciation)	240	240	—
Depreciation	—	80	$80
Earnings before tax	240	160	(80)
Taxes	120	80	(40)
Accounting net earnings	120	80	(40)
Plus depreciation	—	80	80
Cash flow	$120	$160	$40

is used in conjunction with other methods in determining the acceptability of an investment. The prime reason it is used with other methods of evaluation is that payback is not a true rate of return and does not measure profitability or return on investment. To understand payback, it is important to recognize its advantages and disadvantages. The advantages are as follows:

- *Easy to calculate and understand.* Of all the evaluation methods, payback is the easiest to calculate and understand. It merely requires identifying the total of investment dollars of the project and dividing this by the annual cash flows.

- *Indicates cash risk.* As compared to other methods of calculation, payback is an excellent indicator of the riskiness of a project. The longer the payback period, the higher the risk; the shorter the payback period, the lower the risk. In times of a tight cash position, payback will play a major role in this decision. Remember that in a rapidly changing economy the longer you wait to recover your investment, the more risk you face in recovering that investment.

- *Measures recoverability.* Payback measures the recovery period when annual cash flow equals the total investment. At this point, the project is said to be at payback, meaning that your investment has been fully recovered. The importance of the calculation is given only up to the point of payback.

- *Gives greater weight to earlier cash flows.* Because payback is measured only up to the recovery period, annual cash flows have greater weight in the earlier years. Annual cash flows beyond the payback period calculation are not significant for this calculation. Therefore, it is important that a project be structured whereby cash flows are generated more heavily in the earlier periods. Also, as will be discussed later, it will have a favorable impact on other methods of calculating return on investment.

Two of the disadvantages of payback are as follows:

- *Does not represent a true rate of return.* As discussed previously, payback measures at what period the investment will be recovered from cash flows generated from the project. Therefore, it does not measure return on investment, since any method of return on investment would consider the total cash flows for the life of the project.

- *Difficult to compare between projects.* Because the calculation of payback results in a time period, that is, years and months, it is difficult to measure projects on a comparable basis. For example, different types of projects can have the same payback as well as different amounts of project investment. Therefore, the projects assume an equal status, but in reality they are quite different. The only similarity is that they have the same payback period.

Calculation of Payback

The calculation of payback is based on the cash flow projections previously discussed. Referring to the previous calculations, the annual cash flow data (in $1,000s) were as follows:

Investment	0	1	2	3	4
			Year		
Machinery and equipment	$80				
Working capital	$40				
Annual cash flows		$40	$40	$40	$40

Applying the formula for determining the payback period, investment divided by annual cash flows, the following number of years are required to recoup the initial investment:

$$\frac{\text{Investment}}{\text{Annual cash flows}} = \frac{\$120,000}{\$\ 40,000} = 3 \text{ years}$$

The preceding calculation assumes that the annual cash flows are even each year. In reality this will not be the case, because sales volume and costs will vary from year to year. Assuming this variance, the following annual cash flow data (in $1000s) result:

Investment	0	1	2	3	4
			Year		
Machinery and equipment	$80				
Working capital	$40				
Annual cash flow		$45	$50	$40	$35

The payback period has now changed from 3 years to 2.625 years, calculated as follows:

Total investment to be recovered	$120,000
Two years' cash flows	$ 95,000
Remainder to be recovered	$ 25,000

Partial year calculation

$$\frac{\$25,000}{\$40,000} = 0.625$$

Payback calculation

Total full years to recover investment	2.0 years
Partial year to recover investment	0.625 years
Total payback period	2.625 years

Note how much shorter the payback period is when heavier cash flows are received in the earlier periods. It will be seen later how favorable the return on investment rates will be on projects with heavier cash flows in earlier periods.

Discounted Payback

Applying the discounted cash flow concept (to be discussed later), payback can now reflect the time value of money. Assuming the previous data, let us apply a 16% discount rate, with results as shown in Table 7-3.

The discounted payback is approximately 16% over the 4 years.

Payback Reciprocal

One way of relating the payback period to the rate of return is to use the payback reciprocal. This represents a rough estimate of the rate of return where the project's life is at least twice the payback period. It is calculated as follows, using the data previously presented:

$$\frac{\text{Average annual cash flows}}{\text{Investment}} = \frac{\$\ 40,000}{\$120,000} = 33.3\%$$

In this case, a 3-year payback period is equivalent to a 33.3% rate of return. Note that, when the payback period is multiplied by the rate of return, the answer will always equal one.

Accounting Methods

Accounting methods of evaluation can be calculated in many different ways. They can be calculated using the original investment or an average investment. Other calculations also exist. The basic difference between these methods and others that have been discussed is that the calculations are from only reported accounting data and not from cash flow. These calculations will be explained

Table 7.3 Calculation of Discounted Payback

Year	Investment	Annual Cash Flows	Present Value Factors—16%	Net Present Values
0	($120,000)		1.000	($120,000)
1		$45,000	0.862	38,790
2		50,000	0.743	37,150
3		40,000	0.641	25,640
4		35,000	0.552	19,320
Total				$ 900

later. Two of the advantages of these methods are as follows:

- *Easy to calculate.* This method is easy to calculate, because the same data are used as in preparing accounting statements. No consideration is given to adding back depreciation to arrive at cash flow.

- *Ties in with accounting records.* When financial data are forecast into the future for capital investments, they are prepared as if one is preparing future accounting statements. Therefore, in future periods, this forecasted data can be measured to actual performance as compared to forecasts projected into the future.

Some of the disadvantages of using these methods tend to outweigh the advantages, and therefore they are not as widely used as some other methods. The disadvantages include the following:

- *Relies on accounting data.* The reliance on accounting data can create problems, since some accounting principles change periodically, as do certain adjusting entries. This sometimes distorts the projections in using historical data as a base. In addition, a knowledge of accounting is needed, and not all contributors to the input of a capital project may have this technical knowledge.

- *Gives equal weight to all cash flows.* By treating all cash flows as equal entities, all cash flows are given equal weight. No distinction is made for earlier monies, which have more value, since they can be reinvested at an earlier period. This is compensated for when using discounted cash flow.

- *Assumes that project will last its total life.* Because all cash flows must be calculated for the entire life of the project, it is assumed that the project will last the entire estimated life.
- *Ignores the time value of money.* No consideration is given for each of the yearly cash flow projections for the time value of money. Money is assumed to be more valuable in the earlier years since it can be re-invested that much quicker.

Calculations

Using the previous data, the following calculations are made:

Return on original investment

$$\frac{\text{Yearly cash flows}}{\text{Original investment}} = \frac{\$\ 40,000}{\$120,000} = 33.3\%$$

Return on average investment

$$\frac{\text{Yearly cash flows}}{\text{Average investment}} = \frac{\$40,000}{\$60,000} = 66.7\%$$

Discounted Cash Flow

The theory of discounted cash flow (DCF) has been one of the more difficult concepts to understand. By following a logical sequence of events, we will see that discounting is the reciprocal of compounding and that both methods relate to the interest rate.

The basic theory of DCF says that a dollar today is worth more than a dollar in the future. It is that rate, or percentage return, that indicates to an investor what he or she may expect to receive on those funds left to the company to invest over the life of the project. The common denominator for DCF calculations is the interest rate.

Discounted cash flow has many advantages. It provides a basic common ground for all types of projects, therefore providing an ideal method of ranking projects. To measure DCF rate, all cash flows must be included throughout the life of the project. Most important is the fact that DCF assumes the time value of money.

Some of the disadvantages include no relationship to accounting records and the uncertainty of forecasted cash flows. This is extremely important because each year's cash flow will carry a different present value factor. In addition, the calculated cash flows are assumed to be re-invested at the assigned discount rate.

Compounding

To understand the concept of discounting, it is important to understand compounding. Both methods have a common factor—the interest rate. Therefore, compounding uses a compound interest rate that computes a sum of money (principal) at the present to another sum of money at the end of X years. To illustrate, let us assume that you deposit $10,000 in a savings account at 10% interest. How much will you have after 5 years? The results are shown in Table 7-4.

Table 7-4. Compounding Illustrated

Year	Principal	Interest—10%	Total
0	$10,000	—	$10,000
1	10,000	$1,000	11,000
2	11,000	1,100	12,100
3	12,100	1,210	13,310
4	13,310	1,331	14,641
5	$14,641	$1,464	$16,105

One can see that after 5 years, a $10,000 deposit is worth $16,105 at a 10% interest rate. A more simple method is to refer to a compound interest table (Table 7-5) for the compound factor that equals 5 years at 10%.

Rather than going through all of the previous calculations, one could have used the compound factor of 1.611 taken from Table 7-5 and applied it to the initial deposit of $10,000, arriving at the same answer, as follows:

$10,000 × 1.611 = $16,110

The difference of $5 between this result and the one obtained from the calculations is due to rounding.

Discounting

As explained previously, discounting is the reverse of compounding. Whereas compounding shifts the value of money from the present to the future, discounting shifts the value

Table 7.5. Compound Interest Table

Year	10%	12%	14%	15%	16%	18%	20%
1	1.100	1.120	1.140	1.150	1.160	1.180	1.200
2	1.210	1.254	1.300	1.322	1.346	1.392	1.440
3	1.331	1.405	1.482	1.521	1.561	1.643	1.728
4	1.464	1.574	1.689	1.749	1.811	1.939	2.074
5	1.611	1.762	1.925	2.011	2.100	2.288	2.488
6	1.772	1.974	2.195	2.313	2.436	2.700	2.986
7	1.949	2.211	2.502	2.660	2.826	3.185	3.583
8	2.144	2.476	2.853	3.059	3.278	3.759	4.300
9	2.358	2.773	3.252	3.518	3.803	4.435	5.160
10	2.594	3.106	3.707	4.046	4.411	5.234	6.192

Table 7.6. Discounting Illustrated

Year	Principal	Interest Factor	Total
0	$16,110	1.000	$16,110
1	16,110	0.909	14,644
2	16,110	0.826	13,307
3	16,110	0.751	12,099
4	16,110	0.683	11,003
5	16,110	0.621	$10,004[a]

[a]The additional $4 is due to the interest factors' not being carried out to more decimal points.

of money to be received in the future back to the present. To illustrate, let us take the same data used in compounding and apply it to discounting. If you need $10,000 in 5 years, how much must you deposit today at 10% annual interest? Or at what discount factor will X principal equal $10,000? The results are shown in Table 7-6.

Table 7-7. Present Value Table

Year	10%	12%	14%	15%	16%	18%	20%
1	0.909	0.893	0.877	0.870	0.862	0.847	0.833
2	0.826	0.797	0.769	0.756	0.743	0.718	0.694
3	0.751	0.712	0.675	0.658	0.641	0.609	0.579
4	0.683	0.636	0.592	0.572	0.552	0.516	0.482
5	0.621	0.567	0.519	0.497	0.476	0.437	0.402
6	0.564	0.507	0.456	0.432	0.410	0.370	0.335
7	0.513	0.452	0.400	0.376	0.354	0.314	0.279
8	0.467	0.404	0.351	0.327	0.305	0.266	0.233
9	0.424	0.361	0.308	0.284	0.263	0.225	0.194
10	0.386	0.322	0.270	0.247	0.227	0.191	0.162

By applying each of the interest factors, or present values, the result is $10,004. Therefore, given a principal amount of $16,110 for 5 years at 10%, the value of that money today is $10,000. The interest factors in this case are referred to as the *discounted cash flow factors* (see Table 7-7). A simple technique is to apply the discount factor of 0.621 to the principal of $16,110, giving the same answer.

Reciprocal

To further illustrate that compound interest rates and present value factors are reciprocals, let us take both factors for the same period, at the interest rate of 10%, and multiply them by each other:

Number of Period	Compound Factors	X	Present Value Factors	=	Reciprocal
1	1.100		0.909		1.000
2	1.210		0.826		1.000
3	1.331		0.751		1.000
4	1.464		0.683		1.000
5	1.611		0.621		1.000

One can see that both factors, when multiplied, will always equal one, proving that compounding and discounting are reciprocals.

How to Select a Discount Rate

In selecting a DCF rate for any project, consideration must be given to selecting a rate that ties in with the company's objective. Because capital investments will provide future profits with today's cost of money, it is important that the DCF rate that is chosen coincide with the way the company establishes its corporate objective. This would include the cost of capital, the corporate rate of return, the risk potential, industry averages, and so forth. This rate then becomes the minimum rate that is acceptable for capital investment proposals.

Illustration of a Loan Repayment

As previously indicated, the DCF rate is equated to the interest rate. To illustrate this point, let us look at what happens when someone borrows $10,000 at 10% annual interest (see Table 7-8). The repayment schedule is $2,638 at the end of each year for a total of 5 years. The payment of $2,638 represents both principal and interest. You will note that the borrower pays an interest rate of 10% and the lender earns 10%.

Applying this concept to discounted cash flow, we obtain the results that are shown in Table 7-9.

Table 7-8. Illustration of a Loan Repayment

Year	Outstanding Balance at Beginning of Year	Interest at End of Year	Annual Payments	Reduction of Principal
1	$10,000	$1,000	$ 2,638	$ 1,638
2	8,362	836	2,638	1,802
3	6,560	656	2,638	1,982
4	4,578	458	2,638	2,180
5	2,398	240	2,638	2,398
Total		$3,190	$13,190	$10,000

Table 7-9. Illustration of Discounted Cash Flow to a Loan Repayment

Year	Transaction	Cash Flows	Present Value Factors at 10%	Net Present Values
0	Borrow	$10,000	1.000	$10,000
1	Repayment	(2,638)	0.909	(2,398)
2	Repayment	(2,638)	0.826	(2,179)
3	Repayment	(2,638)	0.751	(1,982)
4	Repayment	(2,638)	0.683	(1,802)
5	Repayment	(2,638)	0.621	(1,639)
Total		($3,190)		—

The discounted cash flow rate is 10%, because when the cash flows are discounted at 10%, the outflows and inflows of cash equal zero.

Illustration of Discounted Cash Flow

The calculation of DCF is relatively simple. There are basically two methods of computation, both of which will be illustrated. There are other variations, but these two methods are the most commonly used.

Net Present Value Method

The net present value (NPV) method calculates the net present values of cash flows using a given discount rate. This discount rate is the rate used as the minimum requirement for all capital investments. If the net present values are positive, that is, higher than the investment, then the project is acceptable at that specific rate. If the net present values are negative, then the project is unacceptable at that

rate, since the cash flows, when discounted, are insufficient to cover the investment dollars. In addition, this
method will indicate which projects should be selected
when several projects are calculated. The ones with the
higher net present values would have a higher priority. The
example shown in Table 7-10 illustrates this point.

Table 7-10. Discounted Cash Flow Illustrated

Year	Cash Flows	Discount Factors at 15%	Net Present Values
0	($120,000)	1.000	($120,000)
1	40,000	0.870	34,800
2	40,000	0.756	30,240
3	40,000	0.658	26,320
4	40,000	0.572	22,880
5	40,000	0.497	19,880
Total	$ 80,000		$ 14,120

Based on the $14,120 net present value, the project illus-
trated would be an acceptable project.

Internal Rate of Return Method

The internal rate of return (IRR) method solves for the
discount rate (interest rate) that discounts the cash flows
to equal the investment. Under this method, one is solving
for a discount rate, whereas under the net present value
method, a rate is assigned. The projects giving the highest
internal rate of return are the ones accepted. Also, the
calculated rate can be compared to the overall company
objective to determine the acceptability of the investment.
The example shown in Table 7-11 illustrates this method.

Table 7-11. Illustration of Net Present Values

Year	Cash Flows	Discount Factors at 15%	Net Present Values	Discount Factors at 20%	Net Present Values
0	($120,000)	1.000	($120,000)	1.000	($120,000)
1	40,000	0.870	34,800	0.833	33,320
2	40,000	0.756	30,240	0.694	27,760
3	40,000	0.658	26,320	0.579	23,160
4	40,000	0.572	22,880	0.482	19,280
5	40,000	0.497	19,880	0.402	16,080
Total	$ 80,000		$ 14,120		($ 400)

The residual at the 15% rate is $14,120 and at the 20% rate, ($400). This means that the internal rate of return is between 15% and 20%. Therefore, an interpolation is required in order to arrive at the exact rate. It is calculated as follows:

$$15\% + \left(5\% \times \frac{\$14,120}{\$14,520}\right) = 19.86\%$$

Approaches to Adjusting for Risk

There are many approaches to adjusting for risk. However, the three most commonly used methods are as follows:

- *Judgmental.* Assessing how risky an investment is would depend upon the common knowledge of management. Caution should be taken in being too subjective in the assessment.

- *Adjustment of objective rates.* Each investment would carry a different objective rate, depending upon the riskiness of the investment. Although this is easy to understand, too much is left to the arbitrary assigning of different rates.

- *Adjustment of cash flows.* Under this method, cash flows are adjusted considering the probabilities of each of the cash flows.

Two major drawbacks to the third method are that actually assigning probability levels is difficult, and high and low ranges are not revealed. An example of this method is as follows: Assume a project of $10,000, with a 5-year projection of cash flows of $3,500, $3,500, $3,000, $2,500, and $2,000. Given a current interest rate of 14%, will the investment be acceptable if interest rates rise? By applying the net present value method, the discount factors for each of the interest rates are calculated for each of the cash flows. Results are shown in Table 7-12. The conclusion reached is that, if interest rates approach 16%, do not undertake the project.

Adding another dimension that brings probability estimates into the calculation will validate management's judgment as to the correctness of rising interest rates. Using the preceding data, what is the decision if the probability levels shown in Table 7-13 were established for each year at different interest rates?

Table 7-12. Cash Flows at Different Discount Rates

Year	Cash Flow	14%	16%	18%
0	($10,000)	($10,000)	($10,000)	($10,000)
1	3,500	3,070	3,017	2,965
2	3,500	2,692	2,601	2,513
3	3,000	2,025	1,923	1,827
4	2,500	1,480	1,380	1,290
5	2,000	1,038	952	874
NPV	$ 4,500	$ 305	($ 127)	($ 531)

Table 7-13. Adjusting for Probable Interest Rates

Year	14%	16%	18%	Adjusted NPV
1	90%	10%		$ 3,065
2	90	10		2,683
3	80	10	10%	1,995
4	70	20	10	1,441
5	60	20	20	988
Cash Inflows				$10,172
Cash Outflows				(10,000)
NPV				$ 172

By applying probability levels to expected interest rates, each year's cash flow is adjusted and summarized under the adjusted NPV column. Because the NPV is positive, the project should proceed, assuming that the probability estimates are fairly reasonable.

8

Understanding Your Costs

At some point every business person has asked himself or herself the questions "How much is it costing me to run my business?" and "How much can I afford to spend?" Answering these questions is an essential part of most business decisions. In fact, the answers are probably one of the most important sets of numbers that a business needs in its day-to-day operations. For example, they are essential to knowing how much one's product costs to manufacture and to market. More important, they are essential to the planning and controlling of the business.

Types of Costs

There are many different types of costs and definitions of costs, and each is influenced by a different segment of the business. Some costs are influenced by the nature of the activity, some are traceable by segment of a business, some are associated with products, and still others are based on the passage of time. One can see that understanding costs takes some basic knowledge of the various concepts. The types of costs are as follows:

- *Period costs.* These are costs that are incurred as a function of time as opposed to level of activity. An example would be executive salaries that are paid over periods of time.

- *Variable costs.* These are costs that change in direct proportion to levels of activity. Examples are direct labor, direct materials, and utilities that are based on usage.

- *Fixed costs.* These are costs that do not fluctuate as levels of activity vary. Examples are fixed interest payments, insurance, and property taxes.

- *Programmed costs.* These are costs that result from specific decisions, without any consideration given to volume activity or passage of time. An example would be research and development project costs.

- *Product costs.* These are production costs that relate to the product's unit output and that are charged to the product's cost when the product is sold. Examples are the materials and the labor used in manufacturing the product.

- *Assignable costs.* All costs that are incurred to a specific project, such as an advertising campaign for a specific product or segment of the business.

- *Unassignable costs.* Costs that cannot be directly traced to a specific product and/or segment of the business without arbitrarily allocating the cost. For example, certain administrative expenses must be allocated based on acceptable guidelines.

- *Opportunity costs.* Represents a benefit that is foregone as a result of not using another alternative. An example is the return on investment on other possible project alternatives.

- *Out-of-pocket costs.* Costs that require cash outlays either currently or in the future.

- *Book costs.* Costs in which accounting allocations of prior expenditures were made to the current period.

- *Standard costs.* Anticipated or predetermined costs of producing a unit of output under given conditions. For example, standards are established for material and labor costs.

- *Job costing.* A method of cost system that accumulates costs of an identifiable product, known as a *job*, and that follows the product through the production stages.

- *Process costing.* A method of cost system that accumulates costs by a process or operation as it flows through production.

- *Direct costing.* A costing approach that allocates only variable costs to the product, such as direct materials, direct labor, and direct manufacturing overhead. Fixed costs are treated as period expenses; that is, they are charged to the period in which they were incurred rather than to the product.

- *Absorption costing.* Another costing approach, sometimes referred to as the *full costing method.* Under this approach, both variable and fixed manufacturing costs are charged to all units produced.

Obviously, many different terms are applied to costs, and each is used to define a different controllable segment of the business. Let us review some of the applications by first looking at standard costing.

Standard Costing Variances

As was previously explained, standard costing uses anticipated or predetermined costs of producing a unit of output. Given certain standards, it is necessary to compute the favorable or unfavorable variances that affect the cost of manufacturing the product. Let us look at two of the major items, namely, material and labor.

How to Compute Material Variances

Assume that the standard cost of material is $10 per unit, based on estimated costs from suppliers. Remember that these standards will have been prepared in advance of the actual purchase date. At the time of purchase, we bought 10,000 units of materials at a unit price of $11 because of an increase in the price of raw materials. Given these facts, one can see that there was an unfavorable variance to standard of $10,000, computed as follows:

10,000 units × $11 = $110,000
10,000 units × $10 = $100,000
Unfavorable variance $ 10,000

The material variance of $10,000 is unfavorable because it cost $1 more per unit of material as compared to the predetermined standard of $10.

Now that we have computed the material variance, we need to reflect on the material quantity variance, which is computed at the time the raw materials are used. Assume that 8,000 units were estimated as a standard quantity for production. Actual units used were 9,000. What is the quantity variance?

9,000 units × $10   = $90,000
8,000 units × $10   = $80,000
Unfavorable variance $10,000

One can see that 1,000 more units of material were used, and at the standard cost rate of $10 per unit, an unfavorable quantity variance of $10,000 materialized.

Taking both variances into account, the total material variance of $20,000 resulted because of higher raw material unit prices and more material used in the manu-facturing of the product. In both cases, this comparison was made to a predetermined amount, or a standard cost.

How to Compute Labor Variances

The labor variances comprise two factors: rate and effi-ciency. Together they form the labor variance from standards previously assigned. To illustrate, let us use the following data for both calculations:

Standards
Number of hours	5,000
Wage rate per hour	$6.00

Actuals
Number of hours	5,200
Wage rate per hour	$5.50

Let us compute the labor rate variance first.

5,200 hours at $6.00	=	$31,200
5,200 hours at $5.50	=	$28,600
Favorable variance		$ 2,600

The variance is favorable because of the lower wage rate of $5.50. If you multiply $0.50 (the difference) times 5,200 hours, you will arrive at the same favorable variance of $2,600.

The labor efficiency deals with the efficiency of labor hours actually used versus labor hours estimated. By keep-ing the labor rate at standard, the variance is calculated as follows:

5,200 hours at $6.00	=	$31,200
5,000 hours at $6.00	=	$30,000
Unfavorable variance		$ 1,200

The unfavorable variance of $1,200 is due to 200 more hours having been worked. At a rate of $6.00 per hour, a $1,200 unfavorable labor efficiency rate resulted.

By combining both labor rate and labor efficiency variances, the total labor variances are favorable by $1,400.

Gross Margin Variances

Now that two of the major elements of manufacturing a product, namely, material and labor, have been reviewed it is fitting to explore the variances that affect gross margin. As explained in a previous chapter, gross margin, or net sales less cost of sales, provides the dollars from which all other expenses are to be paid, still generating an adequate return to the owners. It is extremely important to understand what factors affect gross margin and what one can do about improving the gross margin results. This is perhaps one of the most important figures in the earnings statement. Remember that it is this amount that will pay for the costs of distributing the product, general and administrative costs, other operating costs, and taxes, yet still provide you with that adequate return that you desire.

Let us use the following data to illustrate how to analyze gross margin:

	19X1	19X2	Variance
Units sold	75,000	100,000	25,000
Net sales	$500,000	$700,000	$200,000
Per unit	$6.667	$7.000	$0.333
Cost of sales	$390,000	$525,000	$135,000
Per unit	$5.200	$5.250	$0.050
Gross margin	$110,000	$175,000	$ 65,000
Percentage of net sales	22.0%	25.0%	3.0%

One of the key factors is the gross margin percentage. The illustration shows that this percentage for year 19X1 was 22.0% and for year 19X2, 25.0%. This means that $0.22 and $0.25, respectively, are available for paying the other operating costs of the business and for providing an adequate return.

From the preceding data, note that net sales increased $200,000 as a result of the higher volume of 25,000 units and the slightly higher average selling price of $0.333. Because both sales volume and sales price are affected, we need to calculate a sales volume variance and a sales price variance.

Sales Volume Variance

Part of the change in net sales from one period to another is due to changes in the number of units sold. To reflect the impact of units sold on dollar net sales, the prior year's selling price must be kept constant, with units sold being variable. The calculation is as follows:

This year's units sold at		
prior year's unit prices		
100,000 × $6.667	=	$666.667
Prior year's units sold at		
prior year's unit prices		
75,000 × $6.667	=	$500,000
Favorable sales volume variance		$166,667

Sales Price Variance

The other factor affecting net sales is price. By keeping this year's unit sales constant and calculating changes in unit selling price, the following calculation results:

This year's units sold at
this year's unit selling price
    100,000 × $7.00   = $700,000

This year's units sold at
prior year's unit selling price
    100,000 × $6.667   = $666,667

    Favorable sales price variance $ 33,333

Note that, combining both variances, the total change is $200,000, the same amount of variance as shown on the original data.

Change in net sales	$200,000
Sales volume variance	$166,667
Sales price variance	$ 33,333

Cost of sales increased $135,000 because of higher unit costs of $.050 and will be referred to as a *cost price variance*. In addition, unit volume increased 25,000 units and will be referred to as a *cost volume variance*. Because both volume and cost affects cost of sales, let us calculate both variances.

Cost Volume Variance

By keeping the prior year's unit cost of sales constant and reflecting changes in unit volume, the cost volume variance is calculated as follows:

This year's units sold at
prior year's unit cost of sales
    100,000 × $5.200   = $520,000

Prior year's units sold at
prior year's unit cost of sales
    75,000 × $5.200   = $390,000

    Unfavorable cost volume variance ($130,000)

Cost Price Variance

This variance is used to measure changes in the cost of the product. It is calculated as follows:

> *This year's units sold at*
> *this year's unit cost of sales*
>   100,000 × $5.250   = $525,000
> *This year's units sold at*
> *prior year's unit cost of sales*
>   100,000 × $5.200   = $520,000
>
>   Unfavorable cost price variance   ($ 5,000)

Combining both cost variances results in the total cost of sales variance of $135,000, as follows:

Change in cost of sales	($135,000)
Cost volume variance	($130,000)
Cost price variance	($ 5,000)

Summary

An explanation of the $65,000 gross margin variance from period 19X1 to 19X2 is summarized in Table 8-1. Note how each variance previously calculated has an impact upon the gross margin.

Table 8-1. Summary of Gross Margin Analysis

	Variance Calculations	Variances from Original Data
Net sales		$200,000
Sales volume variance	$166,667	
Sales price variance	33,333	
Cost of sales		(135,000)
Cost volume variance	(130,000)	
Cost price variance	(5,000)	
Gross margin		$ 65,000

One can see that an understanding of costs in a business will provide the awareness of, and in many cases the answers to, decisions that must be made in order to remain healthy and profitable. It is not suggested that you become familiar with all the skills of a cost accountant, but rather that you develop a clear understanding of how your costs affect your financial outcome. Such an understanding is a necessary tool not only for controlling your business in the present but also for planning for the future.

9

Using Direct Costing in Decision Making

In the previous chapter, costs were defined in many ways. Two terms were briefly defined that relate to methods of costing. They were direct costing and absorption costing. It is important to understand the two costing methods, since they are commonly used in business as alternatives in the recording of product income and product costs. The basic difference between the two centers on how the fixed factory overhead is recorded in the evaluation of inventory. Under absorption costing, the fixed factory overhead is part of the inventory cost; under direct costing, it is not part of the inventory value. Let us explore the two concepts in further detail.

Absorption Costing

The absorption costing method is the more traditional method and is more widely used. It includes all manufacturing costs, both variable and fixed, to all units that are produced. As can be seen in the operating statement shown in Table 9-1, no identification is made of fixed and variable costs by product. It is therefore difficult to apply any volume, cost, or profit analysis of various alternatives.

Note that no contribution margin is shown in the table. Such a margin is important as a management tool for two

Table 9-1. Absorption Costing, The Profit Company, Inc. Earnings Statement, 19X2

| | Product | | | |
	A	B	C	Total
Net sales	$130,000	$400,000	$170,000	$700,000
Cost of sales	100,000	290,000	135,000	525,000
Gross margin	$ 30,000	$110,000	$ 35,000	$175,000
Percentage of net sales	23.1%	27.5%	20.6%	25.0%
Other operating expenses				
Depreciation	$ 900	$ 2,700	$ 1,400	$ 5,000
Selling expenses	5,700	17,000	7,300	30,000
Administrative expenses	4,700	14,000	6,300	25,000
General expenses	2,800	8,500	3,700	15,000
Total	$14,100	$42,200	$18,700	$75,000
Operating profit	$15,900	$67,800	$16,300	$100,000
Percentage of net sales	12.2%	17.0%	9.6%	14.3%

reasons. First, it will assist you in analyzing product performance and will indicate which products require more effort and which may be candidates for elimination. Second, it gives you the ability to see the impact of alternative decisions on different product lines and on the total company—for example, sales mix, changes in advertising expenditures, alternative methods of acquiring inventory, pricing, and other decisions that relate to product performance.

**Table 9-2. Direct Costing, The Profit Company, Inc.
Earnings Statement, 19X2**

	Product			
	A	B	C	Total
Net sales	$130,000	$400,000	$170,000	$700,000
Variable Cost of Sales				
Manufacturing	$ 90,000	$276,000	$ 98,000	$464,000
Selling	3,200	8,300	4,500	16,000
Total	$ 93,200	$284,300	$102,500	$480,000
Variable contribution	$ 36,800	$115,700	$67,500	$220,000
Percentage of net sales	28.3%	28.9%	39.7%	31.4%
Direct fixed expenses	3,300	6,500	4,200	14,000
Product contribution	$ 33,000	$109,200	$ 63,300	$206,000
Percentage of net sales	25.8%	27.3%	37.2%	29.4%
Indirect Fixed Expenses				
Manufacturing				$ 66,000
Selling				—
Administrative				25,000
General				15,000
Total				106,000
Operating income				$100,000
Percentage of net sales				14.3%

Also note that fixed and variable costs are not identified by product in all of the major account classifications shown in the table. The costs are not period costs but are considered as part of the product. Also note that the manufacturing overhead costs are not reflected in the earnings statement until the product is sold, because the costs are still part of the cost of inventory. This costing method does present some problems in understanding the behavior of costs, because it does not enable managers to simulate "what if's" on the impact of profits using various alternative decisions.

Direct Costing

Direct costing is sometimes referred to as *variable costing* because it applies only the variable portion of production costs to the product costs. This costing method will give an executive a better understanding of how costs behave by segmenting costs into both variable and fixed and by providing a product contribution for each product. As previously explained, this product contribution is a valuable tool in operating the business.

Taking the same set of data used in Table 9-1 for absorption costing, the earnings statement in Table 9-2 reflects a direct costing approach.

Note that the costs are identified by product and are charged in the period in which the costs were incurred. Therefore, earnings are more directly related to sales. Under this method, a product contribution is established for each product, thus giving information as to each product's contribution. Decisions can then be reached as to expanding, continuing, or eliminating a product or product line. This same analysis can be used to measure sales segments such as branches, districts, and regions as well as individual performance for salespersons and sales executives.

Profit Differences

Using direct costing, profits by product will vary because of the timing of the charging of fixed factory overhead to the earnings statement. As pointed out previously, by using absorption costing, this expense is charged to inventory and is not reflected on the earnings statement until such time that the inventory is sold. Therefore, it becomes part of the cost of goods sold. On the other hand, fixed factory overhead is included as an expense immediately, and only the variable cost is included in the cost of inventory when using direct costing.

The two methods will show differences in reported profits as to levels of sales volume and production. For example, when production is higher than sales, higher profits are reported using absorption costing. When sales are higher than production, higher profits are reported using direct costing. Other conditions exist that will also change reported profits under different costing methods. In cases where both sales and production are equal, both costing methods will generally reflect the same profits. Also, over long periods, differences in reported profits will level off or will become less significant.

Using Direct Costing for Decision Making

One may begin to see the many advantages to using direct costing for many important decisions in operating a business. Using this method for internal reporting will assist you in knowing more about your product costs and in the following:

- Marketing decisions to be made relative to sales mix
- Distinguishing differences between fixed and variable costs in manufacturing, selling, general, and administrative costs

- Avoiding the need to establish any basis for allocating fixed expenses and thereby eliminating the tedious allocation of expenses
- Establishing a method of responsibility reporting based on controllable cost data

When using this method for pricing, caution should be taken. Because not all costs are charged to the product, it is important to keep that in mind when applying it to a pricing decision. You may create an underpricing condition because direct costing takes into consideration only direct costs and may understate the product's cost and inflate product margins. You cannot change costing methods to calculate prices, because different costing methods will give you different conclusions. Let us use the illustration in Table 9-3 to make this point.

Table 9-3. Comparison of Gross Margins Using Different Costing Methods

	Absorption Costing	Direct Costing	Difference
Projected unit sales	10,000	10,000	—
Projected unit price	$7.00	$7.00	—
Projected sales dollars	$70,000	$70,000	—
Manufacturing cost	$52,500	$47,000	$5,500
Gross margin	$17,500	$23,000	$5,500
Percentage of sales dollars	25.0%	32.9%	7.9%

The two methods result in differing gross margin percentages. You must take this into consideration when developing a pricing structure for your company. (See Chapter 13 for further details.)

Impact of Decisions

As indicated, direct costing represents an excellent tool for showing how certain decisions will affect the overall profitability of a company. By separating fixed and variable costs, an executive can see how costs behave by identifying product costs. Therefore, it is possible to simulate business decisions by changing various segments for different products to see how these decisions affect the profitability of the company. This planning mechanism will show how best to utilize the resources that make up the product mix of the company.

In order to show the impact, certain decisions will be presented, and increases or decreases to operating income will result. Additions to operating income will be accepted, and subtractions to operating income will be rejected. The data will reflect the earnings statement previously developed using the direct costing method. Let us look at a sampling of planning decisions and observe the impact on operating income.

Assumption 1

You would like to increase indirect administrative expenses by 10%. To offset this additional cost, you will increase the sales of Product B, your best-selling product, by 5%.

Increased indirect administrative expenses	($2,500)
Increase Product B sales	
$400,000 × 0.05 × 0.273	$5,460
Increase in operating income	$2,960

Assumption 2

To increase sales 10% on Product A, you must decrease
your selling price 5%.

Lower selling price for Product A	($6,500)
Increase Product A sales	
$123,500 ($130,000 – $6,500) of sales at 10% increase in sales ($12,350) at a product contribution rate of 21.9% (recalculated using new net sales)	$2,705
Decrease in operating income	($3,795)

Assumption 3

You would like to increase sales of Product C by 20% and
decrease sales of Product A by 8%.

Increase Product C by 20%	
$34,000 × 0.372	$12,648
Decrease Product A sales by 8%	
$10,400 × 0.258	($2,683)
Increase in operating income	$9,965

Assumption 4

You would like to shift the sales of Products A and B to
Product C, which is more profitable. You estimate that
you can shift 15% of the sales of Products A and B, without any customer problems, to Product C, which has an
expanding marketplace.

Lower Product A sales
$19,500 × 0.258   ($5,031)

Lower Product B sales
$60,000 × 0.273   ($16,380)

Increase Product C sales
$79,500 × 0.372 $29,574

    Increase in operating income $8,163

Impact on Operating Income

The preceding assumptions and their impact on operating income are summarized in Table 9-4. It is recognized that, from a practical point of view, all these assumptions would not occur at the same time. However, they do illustrate the advantages of calculating the impact on operating income of "what if" assumptions using data from a direct costing statement.

Table 9-4. Summary of Impact on Operating Income

Assumptions	Impact on Operating Income	Accepted or Rejected
1	$2,960	Accepted
2	(3,795)	Rejected
3	9,965	Accepted
4	8,163	Accepted
Total	$17,293	

The only assumption that should be rejected is Assumption 2, because it will have a negative impact on operating income. The other three assumptions will contribute

$21,088 to operating income. If we were to add this additional operating income to the original operating income, a substantial return on net sales will materialize, as follows:

	Original	Revised	Change
Net sales	$700,000	$725,850	$25,850
Operating income	100,000	121,088	21,088
Percentage of net sales	14.3%	16.7%	2.4%

Additional net sales ($725,850) due to assumptions are shown in Table 9-5.

Table 9-5. Summary of Additional Sales based on Assumptions

Assumptions	Product A	B	C	Total
1		$20,000		$20,000
2	$ 5,850			5,850
4	(19,500)	(60,000)	$79,500	—
Total	($13,650)	($40,000)	$79,500	$25,850

The return on net sales has increased 2.4 percentage points, which reflects the three favorable assumptions.

Summary

What has been demonstrated is the value of using direct costing as a method of simulating the impact of certain operating decisions. An understanding of the differences between fixed and variable costs is a much needed tool for any company. It will assist in many managerial decisions needed to operate the business.

10

Controlling Your Costs

This chapter will explore the various ways of controlling costs. As has been pointed out, effective cost control requires constant review of costs to identify those areas that need corrective action. The key is to identify problem areas and to be able to isolate and direct all attention to those areas so that prompt action is taken not only to resolve the problem but to ensure that it does not arise again. Avoiding waste, labor inefficiencies, and administrative expenses disproportionate to the company's size contributes to the costing side of your company. The sensitivity of the costs of your products to profitability is easily demonstrated by the following illustration:

Selling price	$10.00
Cost of product	6.00
Other costs	3.00
Profit before tax	$ 1.00
Percentage of selling price	10.0%

The illustration shows that, for every unit sold, a dollar will result in profit before tax, or a 10% return for every unit sold. Saving just 1% of the total cost of $9.00, or $0.09, would increase profits to 9%, as shown in Table 10-1. This 9% increase in profits, from $1.00 to $1.09, occurs without a sales price increase or higher volume. One can see that cost savings add substantially to the profitability of the product as well as to the company.

Table 10-1. Cost Savings Illustrated

	Original	Revised	Change
Selling price	$10.00	$10.00	–
Cost of product	6.00	5.94	$0.06
Other costs	3.00	2.97	0.03
Profit before tax	$ 1.00	$ 1.09	$0.09
Percentage of selling price	10.0%	10.9%	0.9%

How to Identify a Cost Problem

One of the most important elements of controlling costs is the identification of the costs needing correction. There are many ways to establish guidelines that will enable you to recognize that costs are "out of line."

Industry Averages

A useful way of determining whether your costs are within standard guidelines is to use industry averages. These averages can be obtained from trade associations, certain firms that report specific financial data by industry, annual reports, 10K's, or any other available source. Many of these data are available as percentages of sales for each of the major expense classifications. In some cases, data are broken down by the size of the business, in such terms as number of employees, sales volume, and assets employed. Comparing your percentages to industry averages will provide some guidance as to where you need to spend some time in analyzing and controlling costs.

Historical Performance

Probably the easiest and most beneficial approach is to observe trends in historical performance. Caution must be taken to use comparable periods before drawing any conclusions. For example, it is best to compare like months, or like seasons, since certain expenses would affect the percentage relationships given different levels of volume. In addition, be sure that you are taking into consideration the same number of working days if sales are dependent on working days. One way to solve this problem is to use the same period, such as a 13-week quarter. With holidays falling out on different days, using a 13-week quarter will generally give you the same amount of working days from like quarter to like quarter.

Percentages

Another way of recognizing excessive costs is to develop a statement that shows percentage relationships between each expense category and net sales. However, you must recognize that certain costs will increase with higher volumes but will remain at a constant percentage. These costs are variable and increase in the same proportion with volume as previously discussed in another chapter. For example, in the earnings statement shown in Table 10-2, cost of sales dollars increased $150,000 from 19X1 to 19X2 due to higher sales volume, but the percentage relationship remained at 75%. In other words, every sales dollar required $0.75 of costs, thus leaving $0.25 to recover all the other costs and still generate an adequate profit.

In reviewing the cost of sales, it is important to determine whether you are in a competitive market with your pricing and whether your costs of producing the product

**Table 10-2. The Profit Company, Inc., Earnings Statement
19X1 versus 19X2 (in $1,000s)**

	19X1		19X2	
	$	%	$	%
Net sales	500	100.0	700	100.0
Cost of sales	375	75.0	525	75.0
Gross margin	125	25.0	175	25.0
Other Operating Expenses				
Depreciation	5	1.0	5	0.7
Salaries—management	20	4.0	25	3.6
Salaries—sales	8	1.6	9	1.3
Salaries—other	7	1.4	8	1.1
Rent	3	0.6	4	0.7
Interest	1	0.2	2	0.3
Bad debts	1	0.2	1	0.1
Advertising	3	0.6	4	0.7
Employee benefits	2	0.4	3	0.4
Payroll taxes	2	0.4	3	0.4
Utilities	2	0.4	3	0.4
Travel and entertainment	2	0.4	3	0.4
Shipping	1	0.2	2	0.3
Telephone	1	0.2	2	0.3
Insurance	1	0.2	1	0.1
Supplies	1	0.2	1	0.1
Other	1	0.2	1	0.1
Total other operating expenses	61	12.2	77	11.0
Income before income taxes	64	12.8	98	14.0

are in line with sales prices as well as those of your competitors. You can draw several conclusions from analyzing the cost of sales. When comparing cost of sales as a percentage of net sales, the following rules apply:

- High cost of sales and prices competitive: Conclusion—the cost of purchasing materials is too high.
- Low cost of sales and prices high: Conclusion—the high prices are creating the favorable low cost of sales and no problem exists in the cost of purchasing.

Also note that, although other operating expenses increased from $61,000 to $77,000, the percentage to net sales decreased from 12.2% to 11.0% due to fixed costs' being spread over more volume, thus reducing the percentage relationship. One can see this in the salary accounts, which are fixed regardless of sales volume. A more favorable analysis would be to measure fixed expenses in total dollars from period to period to avoid the false conclusion that certain fixed expenses as a percentage of net sales are decreasing. In fact, this may not be true. However, over long periods, a conclusion may be reached even using percentages when comparing these figures to industry averages.

Standards

Another method of controlling costs is to establish standards for each element of expense. A format similar to that of an earnings statement can be compiled using realistic standards as to what the elements of the earnings statement would look like in a future period if everything materialized as planned. However, from a practical point of view, there will be differences in certain cost elements as well as in revenue projections. By analyzing the major unfavorable variances, you will begin to uncover areas that need explanation and control.

Controlling Manufacturing Costs

Because manufacturing expenses account for a large portion of the total costs, it is important to concentrate on controlling these costs. The manufacturing cost of a product breaks down into three basic components: direct materials, direct labor, and manufacturing overhead or burden.

Direct Materials

Direct materials represent those that are used to manufacture a product and that ultimately become part of that product. Direct materials can be raw materials, any finished components, or other materials used for the overall completion of the product, such as paint. Most companies know how many direct materials are required to produce a unit. Therefore, the important factors are the controlling of material requisitions and the elimination of waste. Consideration should also be given to looking for cheaper substitute materials or components as a way of saving costs.

Direct Labor

Direct labor represents the amount of labor needed to convert the materials used into a finished product. Labor standards are established for each operation so that an overall labor cost can be developed. In addition, such devices as time and motion studies and rate charts, as well as previous experience, will provide data for accurately establishing these standards. Problem areas that increase labor costs and therefore need controlling are excessive time spent in loitering, inefficient floor layout, tardiness, improper scheduling, absenteeism, poor quality standards, and uneven flow of production lines.

Manufacturing Overhead

These are costs of manufacturing the product other than direct materials and direct labor. They are indirectly used in the manufacturing process and therefore are sometimes called *indirect costs* since they are not part of the finished product. For example, maintenance, machine supplies, janitorial service, telephone service, clerical support, and property insurance support the manufacturing process. Many of these expenses are difficult to control since they do not coincide with volume levels. However, there are guidelines that can be established for controlling these costs. Let us look at these guidelines and some possible solutions.

Labor

The best way to control these labor costs is through proper training and development of your employees. This includes using the right employees for jobs that are in keeping with their qualifications and properly training them in their job functions and responsibilities.

Supplies

Such costs can best be controlled by keeping tight control on requisitioned supplies. Know how long certain supplies should last for their given functions, and always know why they are being requested and how valid the request may be. In addition, always check for possible salvage value of supplies that are being replaced, and look for use in other parts of the company.

Tools

Always order tools that are projected to have long lives. Maintain and repair tools properly to ensure longer life. A major factor in controlling tool costs is to establish policies and procedures against loss and theft.

Utilities

Always practice light, power, heat, air conditioning, and water conservation. Where possible, a utility conservation program should be established that will inform and remind employees of such conservation measures as turning off lights, keeping windows and doors closed when heat or air conditioning is on, turning off unused equipment, and keeping factory room temperatures to an acceptable level.

Other

Other steps such as proper maintenance programs, fire protection, safety, pollution control, and housekeeping will assist in controlling costs and thus increase profits.

Controlling Segments of the Business

Expenses can be more easily controlled by breaking down the business into controllable segments. These segments can take the form of profit centers and cost centers. These centers can be controlled by careful analysis of the activity in each. Even though you may operate a single product operation or a single location, this type of analysis could be valuable even if you establish only several cost centers.

Profit Centers

Establishing profit centers divides the business into business units that are responsible for generating income and that are responsible for cost expenditures. The typical profit center segments shown in Table 10-3 are examples.

Table 10-3. Product Line

	Product			
	A	B	C	Total
Net sales				
Cost of sales				
Gross margin				
Operating expenses				
Selling expenses (list)				
Administrative ex-expenses (list)				
Allocated expenses (list)				
Other expenses (list)				
Total				
Operating profit				

An analysis by region, district, customer, store, department, division, and so forth, can be developed in a similar way as that presented in the table. Each of the profit centers would have its own budgeted revenues and expenses, and analysis could be made at least monthly and, in some cases, weekly. Each profit center would have a responsible individual whose job would be to make sure that agreed-upon objectives are accomplished. The responsibility of both generating revenues and controlling costs would rest with this individual. In some instances, a business may decide to eliminate or consolidate profit centers when activity is too low or when the business changes in such a way that separate centers are no longer needed.

Cost Centers

Cost centers represent segments of the business that incur costs but that do not generate revenue. Without the generation of revenues, individuals with responsibility for profits cannot be held accountable. However, it must be recognized that within profit centers there can be many cost centers. These centers are controlled by establishing cost budgets and are monitored by a total monthly review. Such cost centers include the accounting department, financial departments, administrative departments, shipping departments, and any other support department not directly involved in generating revenue.

Summary

Continuous observation and formal review is required for maintaining the kind of cost control necessary to operating the business effectively. Business executives must be involved in all cost decisions and must review expenses and commitments at all times. Applying some of these basic concepts will keep a company on a sound and profitable basis.

11

Effective Use of Break-Even Analysis

Many businesses rely on knowing what volume of activity is needed to cover all expenses over and above the cost directly associated with the product and/or company activity. To put it another way, how many dollars of sales are needed to cover the company's fixed costs? At this point, revenues generated and costs incurred are equal— neither a profit nor a loss will materialize. When this occurs, the results are said to be at the break-even point, that is, where variable costs and fixed costs equal net sales dollars.

This concept can be expressed in numerical terms by the use of formulas designed for this purpose or graphically, by the use of a break-even chart. In any case, the shifts or changes in revenues and costs are ultimately reflected in the operations of the business. Thus break-even analysis can be an important tool in managing the business by providing the necessary information for effective decision making.

However, certain conditions have to be assumed when using this tool. Because various volume levels will be used to show the impact on the break-even point, it is assumed that changing sales volume will not have any impact on the per unit selling price. It is also assumed that both types of expenses, variable and fixed, will react differently. For example, those expenses categorized as variable will change in direct proportion to sales volume, whereas fixed expenses will remain constant regardless of the volume level.

Defining Types of Costs

In computing the break-even point, it is necessary to take a conventional financial statement and to divide the costs it reports into variable costs and fixed costs.

Variable costs, as previously explained, are those that will vary in direct proportion to levels of activity and that are directly related to the product. Costs that are typically classified as variable costs include costs of materials (raw and packaging), labor (including fringe benefits), shipping materials, and commissions.

Fixed costs are those that do not vary with the level of activity and that remain constant within a given range of activity. They include such costs as rent, property taxes, depreciation, insurance premiums, salaries (not hourly), administrative costs, and general overhead.

Taking both of these types of costs, what impact would production changes have on them? Let us examine the following illustration:

	Total Costs	
	Variable Costs	Fixed Costs
Production increase	Increase	No change
Production decrease	Decrease	No change

One can see that production changes have no impact on fixed costs, but that they affect variable costs in the same direction. However, if we looked at the impact on per unit costs, a different answer would result, as follows:

	Per Unit Costs	
	Variable Costs	Fixed Costs
Production increase	No change	Decrease
Production decrease	No change	Increase

Note that, on a per unit basis, variable costs do not change because these costs vary with production levels. However, the more units produced, the lower the fixed costs per unit, because these costs are spread over more units. Conversely, the less units produced, the higher the fixed costs per unit, because fewer units must absorb more of the fixed costs.

The hypothetical earnings statement shown in Table 11-1 has been arranged to show the proper classifications of variable and fixed costs. Those costs directly related to the product are broken down into variable and fixed costs. Breaking it down on a per unit basis, the variable costs per unit were $4.70, and the fixed costs per unit $1.30, or a total unit cost of $6.00. With a selling price of $7.00 per unit, the operating profit per unit was $1.00. In addition, 67.1%, or $0.671, of every dollar pays for variable costs for every unit produced. However, because fixed costs do not vary with volume activity, the total must be stated in terms of whole dollars. The difference of 32.9%, or $0.329 ($1.00 − 0.671), represents the amount needed for every sales dollar to cover fixed costs. This is referred to as the *marginal income ratio*. We will discuss this approach later.

Table 11-1. The Profit Company, Inc., Earnings Statement, 19X2

	Variable	Fixed	Total
Unit sales			100,000
Net sales			$700,000
Operating expenses			
Cost of sales	$447,000	$ 78,000	$525,000
Depreciation		5,000	5,000
Selling expenses	23,000	7,000	30,000
Administrative expenses		25,000	25,000
General expenses		15,000	15,000
Total	$470,000	$130,000	$600,000
Operating profit			100,000
Other (income) expense			2,000
Income before income taxes			98,000
Income taxes			48,000
Net earnings			$ 50,000
Percentage of net sales	67.1%		7.1%

Break-even Calculations

The basic calculation for determining the break-even point is

Net sales = Variable costs + Fixed costs

The break-even point is reached when net sales equals variable costs plus fixed costs. It is at this point, that is, when both revenues and expenses are equal and neither a profit nor a loss results, that the company is said to be at break-even. The solution can be calculated either in units or in sales dollars.

Break-even in Units

Let us review the break-even point in units first, by using the following formula and the data previously presented:

Sales price per unit (*SP*)	$7.00
Unit sales (*US*)	100,000 units
Fixed costs (*FC*)	$130,000
Unit variable costs (*VC*)	$4.70

$$SP \times US = FC + VC$$
$$(SP \times US) - (VC \times US) = FC \times SP$$
$$US (SP - VC) = FC$$
$$US = \frac{FC}{(SP - VC)}$$

or

$$US = \frac{\$130,000}{\$7.00 - \$4.70}$$
$$US = 56,521.7 \text{ units}$$

The break-even in units sold is 56,521.7 units. To prove that these many units are needed to break even, multiply the units by the selling price of $7.00 and by the variable unit cost of $4.70. Subtract the variable cost from the total sales dollars as well as the fixed costs of $130,000. The result should equal zero.

Net sales (56,521.7 × $7.00)	$395,652
Variable costs (56,521.7 × $4.70)	$265,652
	$130,000
Less fixed costs	$130,000
Total	0

If a specific profit were desired, the formula would be changed to include the desired profit, shown as follows:

Net sales = Variable costs + Fixed costs + Desired profit

Break-even in Sales Dollars

This solution solves for how many sales dollars are necessary to equal the fixed costs. The formula of break-even is as follows, using the previous data:

Breakeven sales dollars (*BE*)

Fixed costs (*FC*)	$130,000
Total variable costs (*TVC*)	$470,000
Net sales (*NS*)	$700,000

$$BE = \frac{FC}{1 - (TVC/NS)}$$

or

$$BE = \frac{\$130,000}{1 - (\$470,000/\$700,000)}$$

$$BE = \frac{\$130,000}{0.3286}$$

$$BE = \$395,617.77$$

The results show that $395,617.77 is needed to equal the fixed costs without showing any profit or loss. This is proved as follows:

Net sales	$395,617.77
Variable costs at 67.14%	$265,617.77
Variable margin	$130,000.00
Less fixed costs	$130,000.00
Total	0

Contribution Margin

This solves for how many units are necessary both to recover fixed costs and to generate a desired profit. The contribution margin is calculated as follows:

Net sales − Variable costs = Fixed costs + Desired profit

By applying this equation to the previous data, the contribution margin is $230,000, assuming a desired profit of $100,000.

$$\$700,000 - 470,000 = \$130,000 + 100,000$$
$$\$230,000 = \$230,000$$

Using the $230,000 contribution margin, or $2.30 per unit, the following number of units are needed to generate a profit of $100,000:

$$\frac{\text{Fixed expenses} + \text{Desired profit}}{\text{Unit contribution margin}}$$

or

$$\frac{\$130,000 + \$100,000}{\$2.30} = 100,000 \text{ units}$$

Returning to the earnings statement presented in Table 11-1, you will recognize the similar data presented in the following proof that 100,000 units is the correct answer:

Net sales (100,000 units at $7.00)	$700,000
Variable costs (100,000 units at $4.70)	$470,000
Contribution margin	$230,000
Less fixed costs	$130,000
Desired profit	$100,000

In this case, the desired profit represented the operating profit.

Profit Contribution Ratio

This is computed by dividing the contribution margin by net sales:

$$\frac{\$230,000}{\$700,000} = 32.86\%$$

Note that this is the reciprocal of the relationship of variable costs to net sales (67.1%).

Margin of Safety

This calculation reflects how much sales can decrease before losses can be expected. It is calculated by subtracting sales at the break-even point ($395,618) from actual sales ($700,000) and by dividing this sum by the actual sales ($700,000). The following results:

$$\frac{\$700{,}000 - \$395{,}618}{\$700{,}000} = 43.48\%$$

Thus 43.48% of the actual sales can decrease before losses will occur. This is shown as follows:

Actual sales	$700,000
Less margin of safety at 43.48%	$304,360
	$395,640
Sales at break-even	$395,618
Total	$ 22

The total, or difference, of $22 represents rounding.

Break-even Charts

Break-even can also be explained by the use of a chart. It is sometimes easier to visualize and demonstrate the relationships between volume, price, costs, and profits by such means. Knowing what these relationships are can be valuable in analyzing business performance as well as in preparing projections for budgeting and planning purposes. Of particular interest is knowing the effects of volume changes, cost changes, price changes, and tax changes on the break-even point of the company. This will be explored later in the chapter. In addition, specific product data are necessary as measures of performance when planning for changes in any of the preceding elements that affect a product's financial performance.

Using the data previously presented, both vertical and horizontal scales are drawn in order to measure volume and costs and profits or losses. The first step is to establish along the horizontal scale volume in units, sales dollars, capacity percent, or any other measurement relating to volume. In this case, we will use dollar sales volume, as shown in Figure 11-1.

The vertical scale of the chart represents total costs and profits, as shown in Figure 11-2.

A horizontal line, which represents total fixed expenses, is now drawn parallel to the horizontal axis, as shown in Figure 11-3. In this case, fixed expenses were $130,000.

FIGURE 11-1. Establishing horizontal scale.

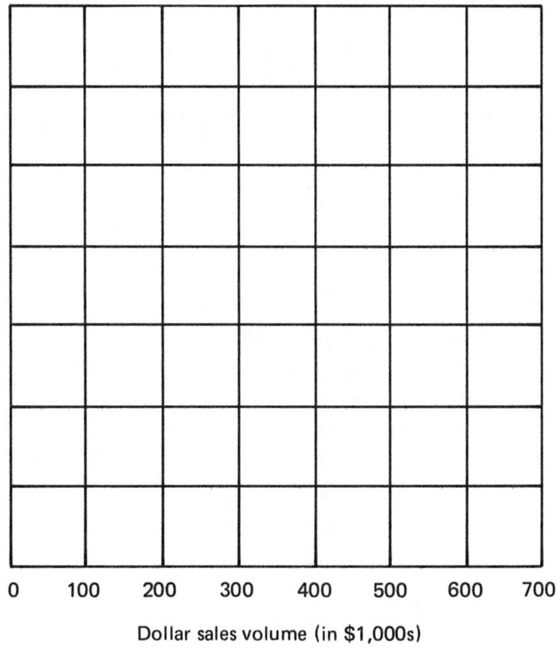

0   100   200   300   400   500   600   700

Dollar sales volume (in $1,000s)

FIGURE 11-2.   Establishing vertical scale.

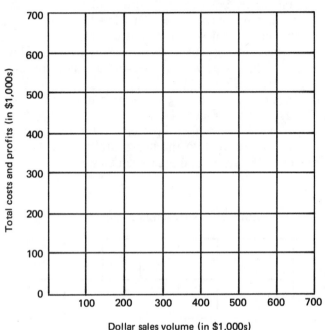

Dollar sales volume (in $1,000s)

In our previous illustration, each unit of sales had
variable expenses of $4.70 per unit. Therefore, for each
level of volume, plot a line upward, starting from the beginning of the fixed expense line, to a point that represents
total expenses of $600,000 ($470,000 variable plus
$130,000 fixed), as shown in Figure 11-4.

A diagonal line is then drawn through the chart,
representing total sales dollars. This is done from the left-
hand corner to the right-hand corner, because the same
scale is used on both axes (see Figure 11-5). The point at
which both lines intersect in Figure 11-5 is the break-even
point. In this case it is $395,617.77.

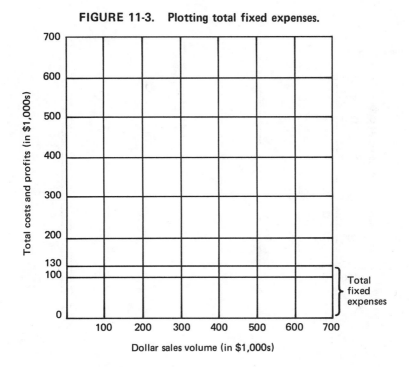

FIGURE 11-3. Plotting total fixed expenses.

How Changes Affect the Break-even Point

As previously discussed, break-even can be affected by changes in volume, cost, price, and desired profit. Changes in any one or in combinations of these will affect the break-even. One of the advantages of the break-even concept is that it allows a business to simulate future business conditions and results and to show how many units are needed to break even. Once this is established, decisions can be made as to the most profitable course of action.

Let us use the same data as were previously used in this chapter to see how the various changes occur. These data are as follows:

FIGURE 11-4. Plotting total variable costs.

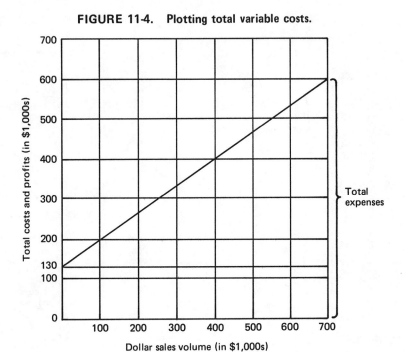

	Total	Per Unit Data
Unit volume	100,000	–
Net sales	$700,000	$7.00
Variable costs	470,000	4.70
Variable contribution	230,000	2.30
Less fixed costs	130,000	1.30
Operating profit	$100,000	$1.00

FIGURE 11-5.   Break-even point illustrated.

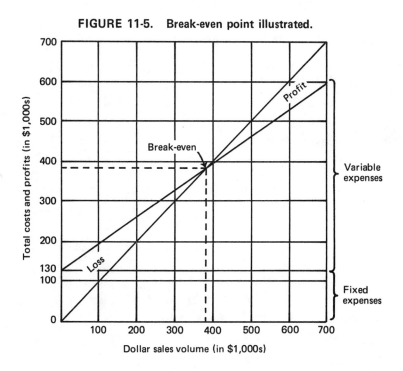

Changes in Volume

What would be the impact on operating profit if unit volume increased to 150,000 units?

$$\$7.00 \times 150,000 = (\$4.70 \times 150,000) + (\$130,000 \times X)$$
$$\$1,050,000 = \$705,000 + \$130,000\,X$$
$$\$1,050,000 = \$835,000\,X$$
$$X = \$215,000$$

The operating profit would increase $115,000, to $215,000. The revised data would be shown as follows:

Unit volume	150,000 units
Net sales	$1,050,000
Variable costs	$705,000
Variable contribution	$345,000
Less fixed costs	$130,000
Operating profit	$215,000

The results show that a 50% increase in unit volume increased operating profit by 115%.

Changes in Cost

Assuming that the same data are used, what would an increase of $20,000 to fixed costs ($150,000) mean in terms of additional units needed to avoid a reduction in the original operating profit of $100,000?

$$\$7.00X = \$4.70X + \$150,000 + \$100,000$$
$$\$2.30X = \$250,000$$
$$X = 108,695.7 \text{ units}$$

An additional 8,695.7 units are needed to absorb an additional $20,000 of fixed costs and still maintain the same $100,000 of operating profit. The original data would now look like this:

Unit volume	108,695.7 units
Net sales	$760,870
Variable costs	$510,870
Variable contribution	$250,000
Less fixed costs	$150,000
Operating profit	$100,000

Changes in Price

How many units would be needed to maintain the same operating profit of $100,000 if the price were increased from $7.00 to $10.00?

$$\$10.00X = \$4.70 + \$130,000 + \$100,000$$
$$\$5.30X = \$230,000$$
$$X = 43,396.2$$

A 42.9% increase in price reduced the number of units to be sold by 56,603.8, or 56.6%. The revised operating profit statement would result in the following:

Unit volume	43,396.2 units
Net sales	$433,962
Variable costs	$203,962
Variable contribution	$230,000
Less fixed costs	$130,000
Operating profit	$100,000

Changes in Profit

What would be the number of units needed to increase operating profit to $150,000?

$$\frac{\$130,000 + \$150,000}{\$2.30} = 121,739.1 \text{ units}$$

To increase operating profit $50,000, an additional 21,739.1 units are needed. The following now reflects the increase in operating profit:

Unit volume	121,739.1 units
Net sales	$852,174
Variable costs	$572,174
Variable contribution	$280,000
Less fixed costs	$130,000
Operating profit	$150,000

One can see how changes in the volume, price, and cost relationships can change operating decisions. The break-even concept allows a business to simulate the impact of these changes. Careful operating plans will assist in reaching the desired goals.

Summary

The preceding analysis points out the flexibility that break-even provides in projecting revenues and expenses under different assumed conditions. By reviewing these data, a company can see how certain actions integrate with the overall managerial decision-making process. However, caution should be taken in regard to certain problems in computing break-even, such as how accurate the revenue and expense projections are, and the extent to which competition will react in an ever-changing market environment. Classifying expenses as variable and fixed can also be difficult, and some reasonable rationale is sometimes called for. Although break-even analysis is a valuable tool, it can be oversimplified to the point where it does not conform to reality. The relationships between volume, cost, and price must be studied carefully and in relation to the marketplace in which the business operates.

12

Use of the Margin Rate
in Calculating Profits

As was seen in the previous chapter on break-even analysis, it is important to establish simulations in order to estimate the amount of volume necessary to absorb fixed expenses. At the very least, total revenues should equal total expenses (both fixed and variable). In order to ensure that revenues far exceed expenses, and to ensure the survival of the business, it is necessary to establish some method of financial control.

Determination of Break-even

To say that your business is successful because it breaks even is erroneous because breaking even does not provide any monies for growth. It is certainly not sufficient for the survival of the business. In the previous chapter, break-even was determined by the following formula:

Net sales = Fixed costs + Variable costs

We saw that, using a sales price per unit of $7.00, unit variable costs of $4.70, fixed costs of $130,000, and unit sales of 100,000 units, the break-even in units was 56,521.7 units.

An easier way to calculate the break-even would be to calculate the *margin rate,* which is $2.30, or the selling price of $7.00 less the variable cost of $4.70. The margin rate of $2.30 is used to recover the fixed costs of $130,000. The fixed costs are recovered at the rate of $2.30 per unit and by 56,521.7 units, as follows:

$$\frac{\text{Fixed costs}}{\text{Margin rate}} = \text{Recovery units}$$

or

$$\frac{\$130,000}{\$2.30} = 56,521.7 \text{ units}$$

The break-even can now be found by using this formula, without any knowledge as to what total sales dollars are or as to what total variable expenses are. Note that the only data required are the margin rate and fixed expenses. For example, if the variable cost per unit increased $0.30 to $5.00, and this cost was passed on to the customer, the selling price would be $7.30. The margin rate does not change, remaining at $2.30.

Computation of Estimated Profits

By using this method, the break-even chart would not be necessary. Those units that are beyond the break-even point, or in the profit sector of the chart, would generate a profit at the margin rate of $2.30 per unit. Conversely, those units below the break-even point would result in losses at the rate of $2.30 per unit. Let us illustrate this point by using the break-even of 56,521.7 units.

What would be the impact if an additional 4,000 units were sold?

4,000 units $\times$ $2.30 = $9,200

An additional $9,200 of operating profit would be generated as follows:

Unit volume	60,521.7 units
Net sales	$423,652
Variable costs	$284,452
Variable contribution	$139,200
Less fixed costs	$130,000
Operating profit	$ 9,200

What would be the impact if 4,000 fewer units were sold?

(4,000 units) × $2.30 = ($9,200)

A loss of $9,200 would result as follows:

Unit volume	52,521.7 units
Net sales	$367,652
Variable costs	$246,852
Variable contribution	$120,800
Less fixed costs	$130,000
Operating loss	($ 9,200)

Unlike the original break-even analysis, which needed data such as total sales dollars, total fixed expenses, total variable expenses, and the selling price, this method has already taken all of these factors into consideration by the calculation of the margin rate. We have been dealing here with only one product, so let us explore the use of this method using more than one product.

Multiple-Product Analysis

In the business world, it is more likely that a company will produce more than one product. To illustrate break-even in such cases, the following product data will be used:

	Product		
	R	S	T
Selling price	$7.00	$6.00	$8.00
Variable cost	4.70	4.00	5.50
Margin rate	$2.30	$2.00	$2.50

If fixed costs were $130,000, what would be the break-even in number of units and sales dollars for each product?

	Product		
	R	S	T
Fixed costs	$130,000	$130,000	$130,000
Margin rate	$2.30	$2.00	$2.50
Breakeven-units	56,522	65,000	52,000
Selling price	$7.00	$6.00	$8.00
Break-even— sales dollars	$395,652	$390,000	$416,000

Let us see how margin rates and sales dollar's can be combined.

Combining Margin Rates

It is possible to combine margin rates and to determine estimated operating profits at different levels of sales volume. Let us assume the following levels for the preceding products in a given month:

	Unit Sales
Product R	60,522
Product S	67,050
Product T	55,600

Using Product R as a base, the margin rate factor is computed by dividing $2.30 into $2.00 and into $2.50. The results are as follows:

	Margin Rate Factor
Product R	1.0000
Product S	0.8696
Product T	1.0870

Each of the products has the ability to recover the fixed costs at the given rates. By doing this, all the product lines are put on an equal basis and can now be combined as if only one product were being sold. Each relates to Product R as an equivalence, and all are added together to arrive at a total operating profit, as shown in Table 12-1.

Table 12-1. Using Product R as an Equivalence

	Product			
	R	S	T	Total
Sales volume	60,522	67,050	55,600	183,172
Margin rate factor	1.00	0.8696	1.087	
Equivalent sales volume	60,522	58,305	60,434	179,261
Break-even—Product R				56,522
Excess over equivalent				122,739
Margin rate—Product R				$2.30
Operating profit				$282,300

Let us prove that $282,300 is the correct combined operating profit by the conventional statement shown in Table 12-2.

Note in the table that the same $282,300 was calculated using the preceding conventional method. This same calculation can be applied to many products but can involve lots of time when many products are used. A more simplified method is to combine margin dollars.

Table 12-2. Calculation using Conventional Statement

	Product			Total
	R	S	T	
Unit volume	60,522	67,050	55,600	183,172
Net sales	$423,654	$402,300	$444,800	$1,270,754
Variable costs	284,454	268,200	305,800	858,454
Variable contribution	$139,200	$134,100	$139,000	$ 412,300
Less fixed costs				130,000
Operating profit				$ 282,300

Combining Margin Dollars

When combining margin rates, as previously discussed, we used the margin rate and the break-even point. In this method, we will concentrate on the elements of margin rates and fixed costs. Using the same set of data, we can calculate the same estimated $282,300 operating profit as shown in Table 12-3.

One can see how easy this method is and that it is preferred over the previous method when break-even data are not necessary.

Table 12-3. Illustration of Combining Margin Rates

	Product			Total
	R	S	T	
Unit volume	60,522	67,050	55,600	183,172
Margin rate	$2.30	$2.00	$2.50	
Variable contribution	$139,200	$134,100	$139,000	$412,300
Less fixed costs				130,000
Operating profit				$282,300

Summary

This chapter presented an additional alternative to estimating profits using margin rates as a base. For companies with limited product lines, or for companies that can computerize these data, this method provides an excellent tool for use in controlling the business.

13

Establishing the Right Price

Establishing the right price for a product or service is a major management function. It is a function that has an impact throughout the entire organization and that can be considered as one of the keys to survival. The ability to maximize both volume and price is unquestioned. Every business, in order to survive in the marketplace, must market its goods and/or services in such a way that revenues exceed costs and that the remainder generates a fair and reasonable ROI.

Factors Affecting Pricing

Management must understand that pricing is a complex subject and that it responds to many factors. For example, the marketplace in which a company operates will determine at what price and at what volume levels customers will respond. Your ability to keep unit costs as low as possible will aid in setting pricing guidelines. You must have the capability of manufacturing and selling the product at different economic levels. You must also be aware of what profits are needed to sustain growth and to move in the direction anticipated for the long term.

Outside influences cannot be ignored. They are at times equally or more important in establishing a pricing structure. For example, governmental regulations, legal implications, technological changes, competitive conditions, and current economic conditions will play a key role in your pricing decision.

Pricing Strategies

When discussing pricing, one has to look at five different strategies. Each of these strategies can be used for different products, different markets, or a combination of both. In companies where product lines are broad enough to apply to a specific market or product, all of these strategies may apply.

- *High price strategy.* A technique whereby higher than usual prices are established on selected products. This can create an image to the buyer that the product is of higher quality as compared to those of competitors. This can be effective in the long run only if the product is, in fact, of higher quality than those of your competitors.

- *Volume strategy.* This strategy accepts low-margin products, with profits being generated from high volume. This is referred to as a "low margin, high volume" philosophy.

- *Psychological pricing.* Pricing just below the next dollar amount to create in customers' minds the appearance that the product is priced lower than it is. For example, $9.95, $25.99, and $99.99 appear to be lower than $10.00, $26.00, and $100.00.

- *In-and-out pricing.* Products are priced high and price reductions occur when that segment of the market that is sought after becomes saturated. It is effective only when there is limited or no competition and when substitutes for the product are almost nonexistent.

- *Typical pricing strategy.* This strategy is generally established by the marketplace in that it is a price that is accepted by the customer as being a fair price. We see this strategy in the pricing of certain items, such as chewing gum and cigarettes. This strategy is becoming less important as inflation continues to rise.

Influences on Pricing Decisions

In setting prices there are several major influences that must be considered. Other influences unique to a specific business, however, cannot be ignored.

The buyer generally has the options from whom to buy, how to buy, what to buy, and what price to pay. Given our competitive society, the buyer is sometimes in a very strong position to dictate how the seller reacts. Therefore, it is important that the seller always examine the pricing policies through the eyes of the customer. Put yourself in the customer's shoes by determining how you would react to a specific price if you were the customer. By doing this, you will understand more about how you should price your product.

Know how your competition will react to a certain pricing policy. It is important to know as much as possible about the competition, including its volume, costs, plant capacity, method of distribution, technology, key personnel, credit terms, and profitability. This will help in determining your pricing policy, including how much to charge for special volume users.

Markup Pricing

An approach sometimes used is called the *markup pricing approach*. Although many businesses use this approach, it makes no provision for the impact on profit of fixed costs. Because it applies the same amount of fixed costs regardless of volume levels, it treats fixed costs as a variable expense. In addition, since profits are considered variable in relation to volume, it does not allow the opportunity to cost a product based on volume. The calculation is made as follows:

1. Determine the cost of acquiring the product for sale. It may be the cost of manufacturing the product or of purchasing the finished or subassembled parts.

2. To the preceding costs, add the costs associated with obtaining the volume, such as selling, advertising, promotion, sales salaries, commissions and overrides, and travel and entertainment costs.

3. Determine the desired profit as a dollar amount or as a percentage of total costs in Step 1 and Step 2. This desired profit is added to the total costs to determine the selling price.

The following example will illustrate the preceding steps:

Variable unit costs	
Production costs	$ 40.00
Selling and distribution costs	20.00
Fixed costs	20.00
Desired profit	20.00
Calculation	
Variable costs	$ 60.00
Fixed costs	20.00
Total costs	$ 80.00
Desired profit	20.00
Selling price	$100.00

Other Markup Methods

As was just observed, the markup pricing method establishes the lowest basic price, given a desired level of profit. This method required determining and identifying different types of costs and adding a desired markup in order to arrive at a selling price. This method is sometimes referred to as the *total cost method,* or *full costing,* and can be expressed in terms of a formula, as can other markup methods. Let us explore the three methods of markup by using the following per unit data:

SP = Selling price
MU = Markup percent—25%
DM = Direct material—$30.00
DL = Direct labor—$20.00
OH = Overhead—$10.00
TC = Total cost—$60.00

Total Cost Method

This method, as previously explained, recoups all costs of the product and adds a desired profit margin (markup) to arrive at a selling price. It is one of the easiest methods to use, but can be misleading because of the way overhead costs are allocated. The calculation is as follows:

SP = $TC + MU(TC)$
SP = $60.00 + 0.25($60.00)
SP = $60.00 + $15.00
SP = $75.00

Incremental Cost Method

This method uses only direct material costs and direct labor costs and puts the emphasis on products that absorb more overhead costs. It also emphasizes the incremental costs involved in producing additional sales units. The calculation is as follows:

SP = $(DM + DL) + MU(DM + DL)$
SP = ($30.00 + $20.00) + 0.25($30.00 + $20.00)
SP = $50.00 + $12.50
SP = $62.50

Conversion Cost Method

This method emphasizes the conversion costs (direct labor plus overhead) and shifts the emphasis on products that have high material costs. By using this method, it is very important to allocate overhead clearly and rationally, since overhead will play a major role in determining the selling price. The calculation is as follows:

SP = $(DL + OH) + MU(DL + OH)$
SP = ($20.00 + $10.00) + 0.25($20.00 + $10.00)
SP = $30.00 + $7.50
SP = $37.50

Note that using the same data for each method results in the following different prices:

Method	Selling Price
Total cost	$75.00
Incremental cost	$62.50
Conversion cost	$37.50

One can see that, in using the same markup of 25%, there is a wide variation of selling price, from a low of $37.50 to a high of $75.00. If you wanted to sell your product to receive the highest profit, you would choose the $75.00 price under the total cost method. On the other hand, if you could not even sell your product at the lowest price of $37.50, then you would have to adjust your markup objectives downward, reduce product costs, or a combination of both.

Although the preceding approaches are acceptable, the more advisable approaches are those dealing with price, volume, and cost relationships. The following method that is described—contribution pricing—will deal with these relationships.

Contribution Pricing

Under this approach, the best price is the one that generates the highest profits, or contribution. It relies on using only direct costs, such as for material, labor, and overhead, and brings into focus the impact on profits at different levels of volume and selling price. The key is to determine the best mix of selling price with the anticipated units you plan on selling, or what combination of volume and price levels will provide you with the greatest amount of contribution. The result, or contribution, will provide monies toward meeting your overhead costs and still add an adequate or desired profit to the business.

Let us look at an illustration that shows how the price, volume, and cost relationships reflect the decision to establish the most favorable price for a product.

Current selling price	$100.00
Current unit sales	10,000 units
Sales dollar volume	$1,000,000
Direct costs per unit	$60.00
Overhead and other costs	$150,000

Given these facts, the contribution and profit before tax are calculated as follows:

Net sales	$1,000,000
Direct costs	600,000
Contribution	400,000
Overhead and other costs	150,000
Profit before tax	$ 250,000

Assuming that you can sell 10% more units at $95.00 per unit, and 15% more units at $90.00 per unit, what is the impact on both contribution and profit before tax? The data are shown in Table 13-1.

Table 13-1. Impact of Selling 10% More Units at $95.00

	Selling Price	
	$95.00	**$90.00**
Projected unit sales	11,000	11,500
Projected sales dollars	$1,045,000	$1,035,000
Projected direct costs	660,000	690,000
Projected contribution	$ 385,000	$ 345,000
Overhead and other costs	150,000	150,000
Projected profit before tax	$ 235,000	$ 195,000

One can see that in both cases a reduction in price of $5.00 and $10.00, with increased volume of 10% and 15%, respectively, does not equal the original pricing of $100 at 10,000 unit sales.

	Original Data	Selling Price Levels	
		$95.00	$90.00
Contribution	$400,000	$385,000	$345,000
Profit before tax	$250,000	$235,000	$195,000

However, a more favorable combination is a $95.00 selling price with an increase of 15% volume.

Projected unit sales	11,500 units
Projected selling price	$95.00
Projected dollar sales	$1,092,500
Projected direct costs	$ 690,000
Projected contribution	$ 402,500
Overhead and other costs	$ 150,000
Projected profit before tax	$ 252,500

Assuming that a 15% unit volume increase can be attained at the $95.00 selling price, other factors must be taken into consideration in establishing a selling price, as follows:

- Can you manufacture or obtain the additional 1,500 units?
- What will be the additional financial burden of adding 1,500 units?
- Are sufficient storage facilities available to house the additional units?
- Are additional personnel needed in manufacturing, distribution, selling, and administration to support the additional volume?
- Is there sufficient manufacturing capacity to produce those additional units?

- Is additional raw material available, and, if so, at what price?
- Will the market support that additional volume?
- How will the competition react to your aggressiveness in a price reduction?
- How quickly can you produce or acquire these additional units?
- Is the product's life cycle on the rise or is it declining?

Using a Contribution Percentage in Determining Prices

In using the contribution pricing approach, it is possible to use a contribution percentage in the pricing calculation. However, it is important to make sure that you review this percentage periodically to be satisfied that it is sufficient to cover all costs of the company, such as interest costs on all borrowed capital, and yet still provide an adequate profit.

Using the previous data, we are able to calculate the contribution percentage, as shown in Table 13-2.

Table 13-2. Using Contribution Percentage for Pricing

		Per Unit
Selling price		$100.00
Direct Costs		
Materials	$30.00	
Labor	20.00	
Overhead	10.00	60.00
Contribution		$40.00
Percentage of selling price		40%

If the selling price of $100.00 were not given, and if it were determined that direct costs were to be 60% of the selling price, then the following calculation would give you the projected selling price:

$$\frac{\text{Direct costs}}{\text{Direct cost percentage}} \quad \frac{\$60.00}{0.60} = \$100.00 \text{ selling price}$$

This results in the following:

Projected selling price	$100.00
Projected direct costs	60.00
Projected contribution	$ 40.00
Percentage	40%

Knowing your projected direct costs and what percent they should be of the selling price in order to provide a sufficient profit is an excellent tool for pricing a product in the short run. Because costs change frequently, this percentage must be reviewed periodically and therefore is not useful for long-term pricing strategies.

Use of Contribution in Determining Break-even

The contribution percentage can be used in determining the break-even in units at a specific selling price. As opposed to using the number as a percentage, it is referred to on a per unit basis. For example, in a previous illustration, it was stated that, by reducing the selling price to $95.00 from $100.00, 10% more would be sold. The data shown in Table 13-3 were presented.

The contribution per unit must be calculated as follows:

	Original	Revised	Change
Units sold	10,000	11,000	1,000
Contribution	$400,000	$385,000	($15,000)
Per unit	$40.00	$35.00	($5.00)

Table 13-3. Comparison Using the Contribution Method

	Original	Revised	Change
Units sold	10,000	11,000	1,000
Selling price	$100.00	$95.00	($5.00)
Sales dollars	$1,000,000	$1,045,000	$45,000
Direct costs	600,000	660,000	(60,000)
Contribution	$ 400,000	$ 385,000	($15,000)
Overhead and other costs	150,000	150,000	—
Profit before tax	$ 250,000	$ 235,000	($15,000)

The question to be answered is: If you want to maintain a profit before tax of $250,000, how many additional units must you sell at a selling price of $95.00? The formula is as follows, where

X equals the number of additional units that must be generated to earn a profit before tax of $250,000:

$$X = \frac{\text{Overhead and other costs} + \text{Desired profit}}{\text{Contribution per unit}}$$

$$X = \frac{\$150,000 + \$250,000}{\$35.00}$$

X = 11,428.6 units, or 1,428.6 additional units

The proof is as shown in Table 13-4.

Thus, if you price your product at $95.00, you must sell an additional 1,428.6 units to earn $250,000 profit before tax.

Impact of Changing Direct Costs

What would be the impact if material costs were reduced 20% but labor costs increased 10%? The per unit direct costs would be $56.00, as shown in Table 13-5.

Table 13-4. Impact pf Revised Data

	Original	Revised	Change
Units sold	10,000	11,428.6	1,428.6
Selling price	$100.00	$95.00	($5.00)
Sales dollars	$1,000,000	$1,085,716	$85,716
Direct costs	600,000	685,716	(85,716)
Contribution	$ 400,000	$ 400,000	—
Overhead and other costs	150,000	150,000	—
Profit before tax	$ 250,000	$ 250,000	—

The profit before tax would result as shown in Table 13-6.

Using the revised data, how many additional units must be sold to earn the original $250,000 profit before tax?

$$X = \frac{\$150,000 + \$250,000}{\$39.00}$$

X = 10,256.4, or 256.4 additional units

Establishing the Optimum Selling Price

Many companies have the option to establish different prices with anticipated sales reacting to the different price

Table 13-5. Illustrating the Impact of Changing Direct Costs

	Original	Revised	Change
Materials	$30.00	$24.00	$6.00
Labor	20.00	22.00	(2.00)
Overhead	10.00	10.00	—
Total	$60.00	$60.00	$4.00

Table 13-6. Impact on Profits of Changing Direct Costs

	Original	Revised	Change
Units sold	10,000	11,000	1,000
Selling price	$100.00	$95.00	($5.00)
Sales dollars	$1,000,000	$1,045,000	45,000
Direct costs	600,000	616,000	(16,000)
Contribution	$ 400,000	$ 429,000	$29,000
Overhead and other costs	150,000	150,000	—
Profit before tax	$ 250,000	$ 279,000	$29,000

levels. For example, in most situations, lowering the price would mean more units sold. Conversely, raising prices would generally not generate higher sales. Therefore, given this very general theory, it is possible to estimate the most profitable price level taking into consideration fluctuating volume levels and fixed costs and yet still maintaining the desired profit.

Let us assume that you have the option to sell your product at the following price levels with estimated sales volume at each level:

Price Levels	Estimated Sales Volume	Estimated Sales Dollars
$ 90.00	12,000	$1,080,000
95.00	11,000	1,045,000
100.00	10,000	1,000,000
105.00	9,000	945,000
110.00	8,000	880,000

Note that the estimated sales dollars range from $880,000 to $1,080,000. This $200,000 range resulted from a range in price of $20.00 per unit and a 4,000 range in unit sales.

Keep in mind that these figures must represent realistic estimates in order for the analysis to be valid. The following cost data correspond to each of the estimated sales volume levels:

Estimated Sales Volume	Variable Cost Per Unit— $60.00	Overhead and Other Costs	Total Costs	Per Unit
12,000	$720,000	$150,000	$870,000	$72.50
11,000	660,000	150,000	810,000	73.64
10,000	600,000	150,000	750,000	75.00
9,000	540,000	150,000	690,000	76.67
8,000	480,000	150,000	630,000	78.75

Note that, whereas the total costs increase with additional sales volume, unit costs decrease because overhead or fixed costs are spread over more units sold. Combining both revenues and costs results in the following contribution:

Estimated Sales Volume	Price Levels	Estimated Sales Dollars	Total Costs	Contri- bution	Per Unit
12,000	$ 90.00	$1,080,000	$870,000	$210,000	$17.50
11,000	95.00	1,045,000	810,000	235,000	21.36
10,000	100.00	1,000,000	750,000	250,000	25.00
9,000	105.00	945,000	690,000	255,000	28.33
8,000	110.00	880,000	630,000	250,000	31.25

Based on contribution, both sales volume levels of 10,000 units and 8,000 units result in the same contribution of $250,000. However, on a per unit basis, the sales volume level of 8,000 units with a selling price of $110.00 is more favorable. This assumes that this volume and price level can be reasonably attained in the marketplace.

In summary, one can see through use of the contribution pricing approach how many variations can create changes in units sold, selling price, and desired profits. Finding the right pricing, cost, and volume combination is not difficult but requires realistic estimates and lots of trial and error. Remember that the data used are not constant over time and must be reviewed and revised to reflect changing trends.

Margin Pricing Approach

Another approach is to establish an acceptable margin rate based on sales dollars. This approach will assist in identifying what price must be charged to attain a desired margin. The approach affords the luxury of simulating different variations to determine various selling prices that will result in different margin returns. In addition, it allows you to vary cost data and to reflect different price ranges. Let us illustrate this approach by assuming a hypothetical business situation.

You are responsible for determining the price of a new product. Based on historical data, you need to generate a 30% margin return based on sales dollars. In addition, selling, administrative, and general expenses average around 20% of sales dollars. The following per unit cost data have been developed for you to use in calculating the selling price under this approach:

Direct material (*DM*)	$30.00
Direct labor (*DL*)	20.00
Selling, general, and administrative expenses (*O/H*)	10.00
Total per unit cost	$60.00

Using these data, the following calculation results:

Total per unit cost	$60.00
Margin desired	30%
Selling, general, and administrative expenses	20%
Remainder	50%

or

$$\frac{\$60.00}{0.50} = \$120.00 \text{ selling price}$$

The proof of this is as follows:

Selling price	$120.00
Less direct costs	60.00
	60.00
Less selling, general, and administrative costs	24.00
	$36.00
Percentage of selling price	30%

You must now determine whether $120.00 is an acceptable price in the marketplace. If it is not, you can lower the margin expectations, reduce costs, or a combination of both. For example, by lowering your margin return expectations from 30% to 20%, the selling price is now $100.00, as follows:

$$\frac{\$60.00}{0.60} = \$100.00$$

Other similar analyses can be developed under this approach.

ROI Pricing Approach

This approach determines the price needed to achieve a desired ROI. As in other approaches, the pricing accuracy is only as good as the estimates used. This approach should be used with caution because of the sensitivity of sales volume estimates and the impact they have on the estimated selling price.

Given a situation where a new product requires a substantial investment, it is often necessary to ensure the business of a satisfactory ROI. Using this premise, the following data will be used for illustration purposes:

Investment	$750,000
Fixed costs	$150,000
Variable costs	$60.00 per unit
Estimated units sold	10,000 units
Desired ROI (aftertax)	20%
Payback desired	5 years

The formula that can be developed for computing the selling price under this approach is as follows:

$$P = \frac{(ROI)\,(I/PB) + FC + VC(US)}{US}$$

P = Price

ROI = Desired return on investment

I = Investment

PB = Desired payback period, in years

FC = Fixed costs

VC = Variable costs per unit

US = Estimated units sold

or

$$P = \frac{(0.20)\,(750{,}000/5) + \$150{,}000 + \$60.00(10{,}000)}{10{,}000}$$

$$P = \frac{(0.20)150{,}000 + \$150{,}000 + \$600{,}000}{10{,}000}$$

$$P = \frac{\$30{,}000 + \$150{,}000 + \$600{,}000}{10{,}000}$$

$$P = \frac{\$780{,}000}{10{,}000} = \$78.00$$

The question that you now must answer is whether you can sell 10,000 units at a $78.00 selling price per unit over the next 5 years. If you cannot do this, you must accept a lower ROI, reduce the costs, or a combination of both. When you do either of these alternatives, you must rework the calculation to arrive at a different selling price. When your revised estimate of how many units you can sell is equal to or exceeds the estimated units sold in the preceding formula, in this case 10,000 units, then you can anticipate reaching the desired ROI.

14

Developing an Effective Reporting and Control System

Managing a business is knowing what decisions to make. Making these decisions requires knowledge of the business, or information. The right kinds of information are found in the reporting system that is established throughout the company. To a great degree, the effectiveness of your company and its operations will depend on the quality of the information that is provided. Quantity is not always necessary, but quality always will be at the top of the list. Lack of quality information has been and always will be a major detriment to any business. It is to this aim that we need to explore the issue of an effective reporting and control system.

Recognized Deficiencies

Most companies will find one or more deficiencies present in their reporting and control systems. The degree of inefficiency will depend upon the severity and importance of each of the elements that will be described. For some companies, certain deficiencies are not significant, but for others, they threaten the lifeline to success.

Excessive Data

Quite frequently, reports contain too much information because of an attempt to have a report or series of reports serve many purposes. A report should contain the right kind and the right amount of data to accomplish its objective of providing the right information. Another cause of too much data is that many reports contain data that belong on reports categorized as "special analysis" or "exception reports." Excessive data will confuse the reader, and the report may lose the attention it well deserves.

Inadequate Presentation

All reports should be presented in a form that is easily readable and meaningful. Too many reports do not contain all the data required to make meaningful decisions. For example, when columnar data are presented, relationships should be shown, such as percentages of other figures, prior years' experience, actual versus budget, and variations. The reader should be in a position to make a decision without further calculations. Accurate designations of dollar signs, percents, head count, units, and so forth, are also important. Of course, the method of presentation, such as oral, written, slides, or video tape, is also important.

Excessive Distribution

Quite frequently, reports are sent to individuals who have no need to know the contents of the report or who cannot take any action regarding the contents. However, there are occasions when reports are sent for informational purposes only. Efforts should be made to eliminate excessive distribution by sending only those reports that are necessary to operating the business. A periodic review should be made to see if reports can be combined or revised to accommodate more than one functional activity.

Lack of Clarity

Frequently, reports are presented that are not clear, not in a simple format, and not meaningful. Such reports do not provide the necessary information for effective evaluation nor meaningful data for decision making. Knowing who is to receive the report will assist the preparer in presenting the right kind of information. Reports must be interpreted correctly in order to become valuable sources of information.

Lack of Coordination with Other Parts of the Organization

With each segment of an organization preparing its own set of reports, frequent overlapping of data will occur. In some cases, even data that are necessary may be left out under the assumption that other segments of the organization are reporting such data. One of the more frequent problems exists in not reflecting published accounting data. Reports sometimes reflect preliminary data before adjustments, and even such basic data as sales dollars are reported differently. It is suggested that some organized effort be made to integrate reports within a company.

Reporting on Results

Reporting on actual results versus some standards, such as forecasts, budgets, plans, or prior periods, requires the use of accurate accounting data. Because accounting is based on generally accepted practices, it provides the necessary information in a reasonably systematic order for recording and evaluating financial data.

These financial data, when compared to established standards, will be used to determine how the company is performing. They will highlight not only how well the company is performing but also what segments need attention. Upon isolating the problems, further analysis will highlight the best way of solving the problem by indicating its potential impact on the financial results of the company.

Objectives of a System of Financial Control

The total system of financial control is considered a communicative tool between superior and subordinate. It is important for a subordinate to know what is expected in financial terms from his or her superior. In contrast, it is important for a superior to establish with a subordinate an objective of financial expectations. This is usually done jointly as a means of overall financial planning and is the mechanism for evaluating performance. This mechanism provides a way by which subordinates are motivated to accomplish the financial as well as the overall goals as productively and efficiently as possible.

This system of financial control reaches every part of the company. It is developed by establishing various evaluation segments such as profit centers, expense centers, cost centers, revenue centers, and investment centers. All activities of an organization fall into one or more of these business segments. They are used in establishing performance standards throughout the company and are designed in keeping with both organizational and/or functional lines. Let us review again the definitions of each of these business segments.

Profit centers are organizational segments of a business where both revenues and expenses are measured. The ultimate results are measured in terms of profit.

Expense centers, as the name implies, are segments of the business that are generally measured by organizational units that generate only expenses or overhead. Examples of such overhead centers would be the accounting department, the legal department, the human resource department, and administrative departments.

Cost centers are measured in terms of predetermined costs, such as a manufacturing plant's output, where costs are measured against predetermined standards.

Revenue centers measure performance in terms of sales revenues, such as a sales or marketing department.

Investment centers are those in which investment dollars are controlled and are measured by the amount of earnings generated from a specific amount of investment.

The Basics of a Reporting System

To be effective, a reporting system must follow certain basic guidelines. These basics must be in keeping with the organizational structure and with the "chemistry" of the company. The following basics are found in effective reporting systems.

Timely Reporting

For managers to respond to changing conditions of the business, reports must be timely, to enable them to make certain decisions on a timely basis. For example, reacting to sagging sales in certain markets requires quick response. Having the right information at the right time will usually assist in solving problems that are time-sensitive.

Close Relationship to the Organizational Structure

For reports to be meaningful, they must relate to the organizational structure of the company. The organizational structure will establish responsibilities for performance, and these performance standards need to be evaluated. Therefore, each individual who is either a responsibility or accountability center head needs a report to measure the performance of actual results versus predetermined objectives. Effective reporting systems measure performance along organizational lines and assign clear-cut lines of responsibility for achieving objectives.

Well-Written and Understandable Reports

A well-presented report has a logical sequence. Such a sequence includes defining the significant problems, presenting solutions to these problems, and indicating the impact of the solutions that are to be taken. Reports should be reliable and accurate, because errors create a lack of confidence. When reports contain financial or other numerical data, they should include both comparative data and some commentary as to their interpretation. In summary, reports should be as short and as easy to read as possible.

Reports Designed for the User

A report should be designed with the user in mind. This includes determining what form of presentation should be made, such as graphs, tables, narrative, statistics, or combinations thereof. If users feel more comfortable with graphs, then graphs should constitute most of the report. Always keep the user or users in mind when preparing and presenting a report.

Elimination of Excess Reports

As companies grow, there is a tendency for reports to grow as well. Sometimes the growth rate of reports exceeds the growth rate of the business. An executive must continuously manage the reporting system as he or she manages the business.

There are many ways to help eliminate this problem. For each report, one should determine whether the cost is in keeping with the benefits. Exception reporting, that is, reporting only exceptions, will eliminate many reports and also keep vital ones to a minimum. Reports should be kept in a summary format, and additional supportive data should be presented on an exception basis only. Periodically review distribution lists for accuracy but also to see if the users still need to continue receiving such reports. Try to combine several reports into one report serving many users. Remember that consideration of such expense elements as the cost of paper, preparation of the report, and the user's time will help to reduce costs sooner.

Other Forms of Reporting

Companies should always consider other forms of reporting instead of the written document. In place of written documents, reports can take the form of informal meetings, formal meetings, telephone calls, visual presentations, and video transmission. The costs of each form must be weighed over the long term in order to determine the best way in which to report data within an organization.

Types of Reports

An organization can have different types of reports in order to serve different needs, such as reports on planning the future, reports on controlling the business, or reports that provide interpretative data for management. The types of reports may overlap and, in some cases, serve a similar purpose. However, they are part of the reporting system and should be used to provide the necessary information in operating the business. The development of these reports should be in keeping with the nature of the organization, its needs, and the "chemistry" of its employees and should follow some logical structure along organizational lines.

Planning Reports

These are reports that deal with activities anticipated for some future date. They may be for the short term or for the long term. They deal with all segments of the business and will overlap with the other types of reports, as will be seen. They include financial reports such as earnings and balance sheet projections, cash flow needs, capital expenditure needs, and general and administrative expense requirements. Other types of these reports include human resource requirements, sales compensation, product and marketing data, warehousing requirements, distribution requirements, security data, and computer information. Thus, these types of reports focus on information dealing with all facets of the business. Other types of reports may be presented to meet the future needs of the company.

Operational Reports

These are reports that are used in controlling the business by highlighting those areas of the company that may need corrective action. For example, they include such comparative data as actual versus budgeted data for sales revenues, cost of sales by product line, expenses by department, head count by department, cash receipts and disbursements, inventories, accounts receivable aging, and capital expenditures status. They inform management of the effectiveness of performance against predetermined standards such as budgets and plans. Once these variations are isolated, corrective actions can be taken. Keep in mind that these reports can be prepared daily, weekly, monthly, quarterly, semiannually, and even yearly, depending upon the responsive time needed to take corrective action. Each set of reports will have its own format and its own time period.

Analytical Reports

These are reports that provide analytical information for interpreting performance of specific segments of the company as well as trends. For example, changes in customer buying patterns, sales mix, break-even analysis by product or product line, changes in the financial condition of the balance sheet (i.e., debt to equity ratio), and changes in product margins are some of the data that are provided by these types of reports.

Special Reports

There are always reports that are needed to supplement the other reports previously mentioned. Although they cannot always be standardized, they do present a very important part of the information flow needed to operate the business. They focus on, for example, share of market, number of employees by department, production efficiency, capacity of plant production, backlog orders, average cost to distribute a product, average sales by customer, average interest rates, percent completion of capital projects, and benefit costs per employee. Reports of this nature must be developed to meet the current needs, and in some cases are presented on a need-to-know basis and only upon request.

Determining Your Informational Needs

To determine your informational needs, you need to ask yourself many questions. These questions will determine the nature and the amount of information needed to operate the business effectively. Many companies can operate with very few reports and use other methods of determining information, such as verbal discussions, whereas others see the need for many reports to obtain the necessary information. Some of the questions you need to answer in determining your needs for information are as follows:

- What types of report formats do I prefer?
- What is the order of priority of information I need to receive?
- What is the minimum amount of data needed?
- In my job function, what types of decisions do I make on a regular basis?
- Do the costs of preparing the reports outweigh the benefits to myself and other recipients?
- How effectively am I able to review and evaluate data contained in reports I receive?
- Where is the best source for the information I need to prepare a report?
- What reports can be consolidated and still maintain the same information?
- Are my reports timely?
- What are the accuracy requirements of reports I receive and prepare?
- Is there any special information I need that is not contained in the reports I receive?

- Are there other reports I receive that should be circulated within my department?
- What reports are prepared by other areas of the company for which I do not receive copies?
- When was the last time a report format was reviewed?
- Are there other individuals who should receive the reports I prepare?
- Given the ideal situation, what additional data would I like to receive that are essential to my function?
- Can I function effectively without the reports I currently receive?

Reporting provides the necessary ingredients for decision making. Timely, accurate, and easy-to-understand data must be available in order to manage a business. Without such information, many decisions cannot be made with any kind of authority. In addition, the possibility exists that opportunities may be lost. The well-managed business operates with reports that provide information that responds to changes in the trends of the business.

15

Developing an Effective Budgeting System

One way of controlling and managing a business is through budgeting. The budgeting process is the catalyst that brings all of the planned activities of the company together in a meaningful set of actions. These actions assist in coordinating and providing the controls needed to manage the business effectively.

Budgets are generally prepared for short periods as compared to long-range forecasts, such as long-range plans. Budgets are usually expressed in financial terms and act as standards against which actual financial performance can be measured. In the budgeting process, all quantified activities are prepared for a future period, and actual performance is anticipated in accordance with budgetary levels. It can be said that the term *budgeting* refers to all of the processes involved in preparing a budget; to the coordination, control, and reporting of variances between actual and budget; and to all the policies and procedures needed to accomplish a company's objective.

Elements of a Successful Budgeting System

To have an effective budgeting system, a company must consider certain elements within the organization.

Structure of the Organization

To develop a workable budget, the organization must be structured in such a way that responsibility and measurable units can be assigned. Each unit must be capable of being measured, with clear-cut lines of authority and responsibility. If you are going to hold someone responsible for budgeted standards, the organization must be structured so that there is no question as to whether an individual is held accountable. In Chapter 10 discussion centered on establishing such measurable units as profit centers, cost centers, and revenue centers. Using these business segments, an organization can begin to provide the structure for establishing a budgeting system.

Reporting System

A good budgeting system follows closely the reporting system of the company. That is, the accounting system of reporting and the budgeting system should be as close as possible in account classifications, methods of accounting for data, time periods, and so forth. The reason for this is that budgets represent future performance. If budgeted performance were exactly as budgeted, both budgeted data and accounting data would be the same; therefore, no variances would exist. However, this is an exaggeration of what really happens. In essence, a budget is a projection of what the activities and the accounting records will look like at some future period. It is therefore important that budgeted data represent as closely as possible the accounting system.

Support of Management

In any well-organized budgeting system, support must be given at the top management level for the system to be effective. If you operate your organization with many different operating units, it is important that the organization know that you will use budgeting as a tool for measuring performance. By being involved in establishing the budgeting concepts and procedures, as well as in reviewing budgeted variations, you will lend support to the rest of the organization and create an acceptance of the budgeting system throughout.

Budgeting Definitions

Within the budgeting process, many different terms are used to express either some or all of the activities of a company. Some of these terms are used interchangeably, whereas others relate to specific activities. Let us review some of the terms that are commonly used in the business community.

A *budget* represents a formal expression of the plans and objectives of management and of its ideas and expectations for all activities of the company's operation for a specific period.

Budgeting refers to the entire process of budget preparation, including the planning, coordination, controlling, reviewing, and reporting processes.

A *forecast* is a projection of activity for a specified period.

Financial budgets budget activity that relates to the balance sheet and the company's financial condition as of a specified period. Cash budgets, balance sheet budgets, and capital expenditures budgets are all considered financial budgets.

Operating budgets provide an estimate of activity whereby both income and expenses are involved and are closely associated with the elements of the earnings statement. Sales budgets, administrative budgets, manufacturing budgets, and human resource budgets are types of operating budgets.

Benefits of a Budgeting System

The budgeting process provides an organization with both tangible and intangible benefits. The benefits of using budgeting effectively throughout the organization will enhance the management process. An effective budgeting system will play a major role not only in improving profits but also in maintaining the necessary management process for continued growth. The following benefits result from using the budgeting process.

Involvement of All Employees

The budgeting process involves all levels of the organization. With the support of top management, each operating level must provide the goals and objectives for which it is to be held accountable in keeping with overall company goals and objectives. By having all levels participating in the establishment of goals and objectives, the organization will develop and build a team process of managing the business.

Measurement of Organizational Centers

As pointed out previously, budgets usually follow the organizational lines of a company. Responsibility and accountability centers are established for control, and budgets are developed to meet the performance standards that are necessary to manage the business effectively.

Enhancement of the Thought Process

The development of budgets by accountability heads creates a healthy thought process within the organization. By requesting that each accountability center provide a logical sequence of events toward stated objectives, the thought process of managing that segment of the business is enhanced. In addition, the goals and objectives that are developed and to which a center is committed are usually coordinated with those of the other parts of the organization, so that overall objectives are in harmony with the total organization. This type of thought process provides the ingredients for a successful and well-managed company.

Establishment of Required Goals

The budgeting process establishes the required goals that are acceptable to managing the company. These goals center around the most economical use of the resources of the company, such as capital resources, fixed assets, working capital, and human resources. With these objectives in place, performance evaluations can be measured against budgeted standards, and adjustments can be made to changing conditions.

Limitations of a Budgeting System

As with any management process, certain limitations must be recognized. These limitations can be minimized by the continuous support of top management in providing a workable environment in which the budgeting process can operate. The extent of each of these limitations will depend upon the company and upon the attitude of managers toward making a sincere effort to use budgeting as a management tool. Let us review some of these limitations.

Inability to Measure Nonquantitative Results

Most budgets are developed to measure results in quantitative terms, such as units and dollar amounts. This serves as a vehicle for measuring against actual results in developing corrective actions based on variances. However, certain key management activities are difficult to measure in quantitative terms and may go unrecognized. These activities include the ability to manage a given function, responsiveness to decisions, meeting commitments, developing staff, and overall management abilities.

Dependence upon Accuracy of Input

Budgeting the business can only be as good as the estimates that go into each segment of the budget. If estimates or forecasts are not realistic, then a great deal of effort is expended in finding out the nature of the variances. In addition, many decisions will be made on the basis of the accuracy of the budgeted data, and extreme inaccuracies may generate unsound management decisions.

Inability to Replace Experience

Too frequently, budgets are looked upon as replacements for management judgment. They are intended to be merely operating guidelines and should not be considered a replacement for management's judgment and working experience.

Stagnancy

With ever-changing business and economic conditions, budgets must be flexible to meet these changes. Operational decisions, budgeting techniques, budgeting methodology, and procedures must be continuously reviewed, modified where necessary, and either replaced or continued as part of the budgeting system.

Lack of Support

When a budgeting system operates without the support of top management, response by the rest of the organization is often lacking. As indicated previously, a budgeting system must be supported not only by top management but also at all levels throughout the organization. If this support is lacking, budgeting becomes merely an exercise in numerical gymnastics, and the desired goals and objectives will not have much of a chance of being accomplished.

Budgeting as Intimidation

In many organizations the term *budgeting* prompts a negative reaction. It is sometimes thought of as an infringement on one's personal ability to manage the business, since it requires a commitment and establishes performance standards. Budgeting must be looked upon as a necessary tool to help responsibility heads perform more effectively; it should not be looked upon as a way to stifle initiative. This misconception can be overcome by better communications to help managers understand how budgeting can assist them in accomplishing their required goals.

Methods of Developing a Budgeting System

An organization can develop many different approaches to operating a budgeting system. Each of the approaches is a sound management practice, but some operate more effectively in particular types of organizations. Each company must work with the approach that is best suited to its needs, taking into consideration the nature of the organization, the reporting structure, the personnel involved, the complexities of the budgeting process, and the political nature of the organization. Each of these factors will determine which approach to use, and in fact a combination of approaches may be more effective.

Top-down Method

This method utilizes a central staff that reflects and determines the corporate goals. The budgets are generated by the central staff, and allocations are made to other parts of the organization for profit, expense, and investment objectives. This method has the advantages of simplifying the budgeting process and ensuring that all corporate goals are always reflected. However, it also has several disadvantages. It assumes that there is extensive knowledge of all data needed to prepare the budget within every part of the organization. This assumption generally is not valid, since personnel at the operating level will usually be better prepared and more knowledgeable about what commitments can be made for that segment of the company in future periods. If operating personnel do not have an input into the budgeted commitments, there may be a lack of support for and commitment to the entire operating budget. Most effective budgeting systems try to develop firm budgeted commitments on which performance is based.

Bottom-up Method

This method starts from the bottom or operating level and is based on the goals and objectives for each segment of the company. However, the broad, overall company objectives must be met in developing each of the commitments at the operating level. These overall goals and objectives include such guidelines as economic indexes, tax rates, pricing policies, expense allocations, minimum ROI rates, growth rates, salary policies, and human resource requirements. The way the budget is prepared in terms of procedures and formats is also included.

The process of review and revision takes place at each higher level. This method provides for participation and commitment at each operating level and provides each level with a greater understanding of the business in which it operates. The biggest disadvantage is the time it takes to prepare the many detailed schedules needed to support the budget. Quite often, operating units hold back on attainable performance in order to protect their performance records. They will tend to be somewhat conservative in revenues and excessive in expense projections. Without proper review, not all the corporate goals may be included in an operating unit's projections.

A Combination Method

Sometimes a more effective approach is to use a combination of the top-down and bottom-up methods. Under this method, the operating units would use a bottom-up approach, and feedback and approval would come from corporate managers using the top-down method. Another variation uses certain objectives established at the corporate level and submitted to the operating managers (top-down) and budgets prepared based on operating-level objectives and submitted to corporate managers (bottom-up). The approval or disapproval would then be filtered back to operating managers (top-down), and the process would continue for any further actions.

Types of Budgets

Because budgeting is a "master plan" of the business activities that can be reasonably expected in both the short and the long term, it provides the means of coordinating all of the plans of the company by level of responsibility. These plans involve activities of sales, production, investments, and supporting services. The preparation of individual budgets provides the mechanism for detecting problems that may arise. These problems are usually shown as budget variances, that is, deviations of actual performance from budgeted performance. Analyzing the variances will indicate what corrective action can be taken at that time. To assist in analyzing the business, certain types of budgets are prepared. However, keep in mind that additional budgets may be necessary to meet other operational needs. Therefore, the budgets that are presented here constitute only a guideline for developing a total budgeting process.

Sales Budget

The sales budget requires the development of a sales forecast. This forecast indicates how many new orders and shipments will be made during the budget year. In order to develop an accurate sales forecast, you must take into account your own past experience, economic and market conditions, and the marketing policies and objectives of the company. Let us review each of the major components involved in developing a sales forecast.

Past Experience

Data based on past experience are to be found in internal accounting records. These records will tell you to whom you sold what product, in what location, by what salesperson, the customer's industry, the quantity sold, the unit price, and the total value of the order.

Economic and Market Conditions

These data are accumulated from outside sources and evaluate industry expectations, governmental regulations that may affect your business, consumer buying patterns, and general economic conditions. Certain economic indexes that have an impact upon the business should be isolated and watched carefully. For example, if your products are sold to homeowners, you would be particularly interested in conditions surrounding the housing industry.

Marketing Policies and Objectives

These data deal with the overall marketing and sales objectives of a company. Attention must be given to whether the market share will increase or decrease, to pricing policies, to expanding or contracting of specific product lines, and to overall competitive strategy. You will also want to review some of the product's characteristics, such as its profitability, how the product compares with that of your competitor, the sales trend patterns (to determine at what stage the product is in its life cycle), and how the product's sales volume reacts to advertising and promotional campaigns.

Manufacturing Budget

This budget is closely related and tied in to the sales budget. Supporting the overall manufacturing budget are supplemental schedules or budgets for inventory, production, direct labor, and overhead. Let us review these supplemental schedules individually.

Inventory Budget

Inventories are divided into raw materials, work-in-process, and finished goods. Levels of inventory should be established in relation to not only anticipated sales volume but also many other factors, which constitutes the establishment of an overall company inventory policy. These factors must weigh heavily in determining the level of inventory that should be kept on hand. They are as follows:

- What are the risks of carrying inventories in relation to the marketplace and to economic conditions?
- What is the possibility of storing additional raw materials?
- What are the storage costs of carrying the inventory?
- Does the product have a shelf life, and if so, how long?
- Do the raw materials have a limited life before they are converted into a finished product?
- What is the availability of the raw materials and at what expected cost?
- How do we time the needs of the factory for materials so as not to create shortages?
- How economical is purchasing in large shipments in order to obtain quantity discounts?
- What are the capital requirements needed to finance the inventory?

Production Budget

The production budget is coordinated with the sales budget in determining at what time and how many additional units of inventory must be produced. This decision is made within company policies set forth before the production plan can be formulated. For example, when a product is manufactured, it is based on the company's delivery policy and on the level of delivery performance desired. It is also based on balancing the cost of carrying inventory with the cost of acquiring inventory. Therefore, the production budget is developed within the following guidelines in an effort to meet the anticipated demand:

- The inventory carry cost (interest, insurance, etc.)
- Delivery time requirements
- Level of delivery performance
- Acceptable changes in production employment

The decisions regarding how much material to buy and when are often calculated by the use of a mathematical technique called the *economic order quantity* (EOQ). This technique provides for an order quantity that will produce the lowest possible cost. Therefore, the cost of acquiring inventory is related to the carrying costs of inventory. As the number of orders that are placed is reduced, the cost of ordering is reduced. However, the cost of carrying the inventory is increased.

The calculation considers the cost of placing an order, the rate of annual sales, the unit cost, and the carrying cost of the inventory. The formula is as follows:

$$EOQ = \sqrt{[(2 \times AS \times PC)/(UC \times CC)]}$$

The square root is used on the following components of the formula:

AS = Annual units sales
PC = Procurement cost
UC = Unit cost
CC = Carrying cost per unit

The reorder point (EOQ) is determined by the difference between the time replacement that is necessary and the delivery lead time, given an average demand. To allow for heavier than average demands and longer lead times, some additional stock is added as a safety requirement.

Direct Labor Budget

This budget determines both in head count and in dollars the amount of personnel needed to fulfill the requirements as set forth in the production budget. Using historical records of labor hours needed to produce a unit of production will assist you in this projection. To determine the total direct labor hours, multiply the number of units to be produced by the labor time per unit. Multiply this amount by the rate structure used, such as hourly rate or unit rate.

Overhead Budget

This budget does not fluctuate with levels of activities. It includes such expense items as salaries and wages, overtime, employee benefits, supplies, utilities, and depreciation. In budgeting those expenses for production departments, a measurement base must be established to reflect variances. Some of these bases include direct labor hours, machine hours, consumption of material, and units produced. For example, in measuring the effectiveness of a maintenance department, direct maintenance hours can be used.

Operating Budget

This includes such budgets as advertising and sales promotion budgets, human resource budgets, and administrative budgets. Each of these budgets is prepared by functional areas of responsibility and/or by program, as in the case of an advertising campaign.

Human Resource Budget

This budget provides the human resource requirements of the company and includes such data as head count, salaries and wages, overtime, taxes, employee benefits, training and development expenses, and other expenses associated with personnel. These data are presented by each function of the organization and in some cases may represent data by individual.

Administrative Budget

This budget reflects all the expenses of departments or segments of the business classified as administrative. They include such expenses as salaries and wages, employee benefits, travel and entertainment, memberships, subscriptions, training and development, and office supplies. These budgets coincide with organizational lines and therefore are departmental in nature. Because these departments generally do not produce income, thorough review must be made of each expense element. An exception might be the treasury department, in which revenues are generated through short- and long-term investments. Particular attention must be given to justifying these expenses with the overall plans to service the operating departments of the company. This is one budget that is sometimes difficult to control since profitability is undeterminable.

Cash Budget

The cash budget provides one of the most important forecasts in operating the business. It highlights the operating cash requirements from every part of the organization. It indicates whether outside financing is necessary, or whether money is available from internal sources to meet the cash demands of the company. Such cash demands as investments in fixed assets, inventories, and accounts receivable may require short-term financing. It will also reflect operating expenditures, including financing repayments, tax payments, and dividend payments, as well as revenues to be received from various sources throughout the company.

There are two commonly used methods for developing cash budgets. They are the cash receipts and disbursements method and the adjusted income method. Both of these methods forecast the cash requirements of the company. Let us review each method.

Cash Receipts and Disbursements Method

Under this method, forecasts of cash are traced through all the items of both income and expense. It is a valuable tool in that it gives a complete picture of the cash requirements of the company and reflects the timing of the estimated cash receipts and cash disbursements. The one disadvantage of using this method is that it does not create an awareness of growing receivables and inventories.

Cash receipts are based on sales forecasts and other income items, such as interest income, which are taken from other budgets. Cash disbursements are based on estimated cash expenditures from operations and proposed capital expenditures. Such disbursements will arise from payroll and related expenses, accounts payable, administrative expenses, selling and advertising expenses, production, bank loan repayments, and so forth.

Adjusted Income Method

This method is a longer term projection and adjusts net earnings to a cash basis by adding or subtracting all transactions that affect or that do not affect actual cash. For example, depreciation is added to net earnings in converting back to a cash basis since depreciation is considered a noncash item. This method has the advantage of indicating growing demands of needed financing for receivables and inventories and possible extension of payables. In addition, excess cash will become visible for investment purposes.

Operational Decisions

In both of these methods many operational decisions will be highlighted. They are as follows:

- Operating cash requirements
- The need for short-term financing
- Reducing excessive investments in working capital
- The amount of and the need for investing any surplus cash
- The management of both dividend and tax payments
- The need to take advantage of cash discounts
- The scheduling of major expenditures, such as for capital investments
- The need and impact of mergers and acquisitions
- Long-term financing needs
- The need for developing new products

Capital Expenditure Budget

This is a budget in which proposed capital investments are presented to management for approval. These are investments in the company that involve large sums of money over long periods. These investments in capital assets usually provide the future profits of the company. They also include any additional working capital requirements needed during the life of the project.

Policy Statement

This statement should be included in the capital expenditure budget to reflect any major changes and directions in the operations of the company. A brief statement should also be included as to the general economic outlook and its affect on the company's products. Financial data that should also appear include the costs and availability of money to the company, the required minimum rates of return, and how much in funds is allocated for each operating unit.

Definitions

Included should be definitions of what constitutes a capital project; classifications of projects, such as cost reduction, expansion, growth, and so forth; the treatment of underruns and overruns; intracompany and intercompany pricing; depreciation method used; tax rates; transfer of assets; and the treatment of rentals and leases. Other definitions should be included in keeping with the type of company and its needs.

The dollar limits in referring to *levels of authorizations and who is responsible* for the preparation and control of the contents of the capital budgets must be defined. Other logistics as to where the capital budgets should be submitted, assembled, organized, and analyzed also need to be defined.

The capital budget should indicate in detail such *procedural elements* as forms, instructions, supplemental data, time periods, length of budget period, project classifications, priority status, financial requirements (such as working capital and operating expenses), and treatment of carry-overs and carry-forwards.

Details as to when *reviews and approvals* will take place, as well as those responsible for such activities, need to be discussed. Any feedback procedures and revisions must also be highlighted.

Because capital projects provide future earnings, a capital budgeting program must be designed to give a company the opportunity to earn sufficient dollars to recover the initial investment over a relatively reasonable period. Chapters 6 and 7 dealt with this subject in more detail.

Putting Budgeting to Use

To be effective, a budgeting system must rest on a sound organizational structure coupled with clear-cut lines of authority and responsibility. Budgets should follow these organizational lines as well as individual responsibilities. For a budgeting system to be fully effective, there must be an accounting system that follows the organizational structure with assigned responsibilities so that individual performance can be evaluated. Therefore, the successful budgeting process requires close coordination between the accounting function and the budgeting program. The recording of accounting data (historical) is used as a method of control for current operations (budget).

Meaningful reports must be developed to analyze and interpret the variations of actual versus budgeted data. In addition, supplemental budget reports are designed to give operating managers information that is necessary to operate the business effectively.

The Budget Organization

The assigned budget officer is responsible for designing the budget program and for providing technical assistance and advice to line personnel in developing and implementing the budgeting program. The line responsibilities include preparation of the budget as set forth by the budget officer and enforcement and control of the plans contained in the budgeting program.

Role of the Budget Officer

As previously explained, the budget officer is responsible for coordinating all the budget estimates that have been developed by the line organization and for providing the necessary technical assistance in the preparation of certain budget reports. The function can be further defined as follows:

- To act as advisor on budgeting matters to the chief executive, budget committee, and others
- To recommend procedures and other requirements for each component of the budgeting system
- To develop the organization of the budgeting program and the timetables thereof
- To develop the forms, schedules, and other documentation necessary for completion of the budget
- To develop a budget manual
- To supply some analytical data for operating units to use in their preparation
- To provide key executives with certain revenue and cost data, as tabulated in the budgets
- To recommend certain courses of action to top management, based on budget projections
- To analyze and interpret variations between actual and budgeted results
- To prepare and distribute the budgets

Role of the Budget Committee

Where feasible, a budget committee should be appointed, made up of members of the organization, such as the president, the chief operating officer, certain staff and/or operational vice presidents, the chief financial officer, and the budget director. Although not all of these members of the organization need be part of the budget committee, as many as possible should form such a committee. A chairperson should be appointed, whose responsibilities are to carry out the function of the budget committee. The responsibilities and duties of this committee include the following:

- Reviewing budgeted estimates from each part of the organization and making recommendations to the respective responsibility heads
- Resolving budgetary conflicts between operating units of the company
- Recommending and approving changes to the budgeting process
- Reviewing and making recommendations on periodic performance reports, which compare budgetary standards to actual performance
- Approving the content of the budget manual

One can see that the makeup of the budget committee and its responsibilities will add credibility to the budgeting program. Under this arrangement, the organization will respond to the importance of the budgeting process as an operating tool.

Content of the Budget Manual

One of the tools that brings together all of the aspects of the budgeting program is the budget manual. It is a statement of the approved budget policies and procedures of the company. Like other operating manuals of a company, the budget manual contains all the data needed for preparing a budget. The budget manual should include the following:

- A statement from the chief operating officer as to the objectives and the potential of the budgeting program to the company
- Instructions and necessary forms to be used

- Responsibility levels for developing the input
- A budget calendar that specifies on what dates the data must be completed, reviewed, and submitted
- Administrative details as to how the budget is to be prepared, number of copies to be submitted, and to whom copies are to be sent
- Types of performance reports to be prepared and their content
- Responsibility levels for taking corrective actions
- Follow-up procedures

Summary

An effective budgeting system involves the total organization. It is a total management process, dealing not only with the mechanics and techniques but also with the human factor. Such elements as the organizational structure, the delegation of certain responsibilities and authority, and communications are all part of this management process and are found in the construction and preparation of the budgeting process. Remember that the budgeting process, if done correctly, will coordinate all functions of an organization and direct all efforts toward reaching the desired objectives. It will also assist managers in taking corrective actions necessary to reaching those objectives when there are substantial variances from budgeted standards.

16

How to Develop a Practical Business
Plan

A business plan is designed to provide the business manager with a workable tool with which to operate the
business. Like the budgeting process, it is a process that is
part of any well-organized and well-managed business. A
business plan will assist you in accomplishing the following objectives:

- It establishes both objectives and responsibilities by
  managerial level. This creates a more detailed analysis
  of an operating manager's functions and responsibilities and focuses attention on the total environment
  of the function and not just a segment of the business.

- As business plans are developed, it provides a mechanism of control on the future performance of a
  manager against planned objectives and goals.

- For an organization to move ahead in an organized
  manner, all parts of the organization must know of
  the objectives and goals of the company and must
  work as a unified body in reaching longer term
  objectives. This is accomplished through the business
  plan, which acts as a communicative device for the
  entire organization as to what is expected and to
  what extent each segment of the organization must
  contribute.

- A business plan will often determine the feasibility of current operational decisions and their impact on longer term goals and objectives, since, in many cases, longer term results are an extension of current operating policies.
- The business plan develops managers' thinking process by forcing them to seek alternative solutions and to be flexible in response to the changing conditions of the business.

Determining the Nature of the Business

The first step in developing the business plan is to define the type of business you are in or your business philosophy. The philosophy will spell out how you operate your business and in many cases define what business you are actually in. Many companies find it very difficult to define their business philosophy. Here are some questions to help you define the nature of your business:

- To whom do I sell my product?
- Am I service- or consumer-oriented, or both?
- Do I sell domestically, internationally, or both?
- Is my business cyclical? If so, what are my up periods and what are my down periods?
- How does my product/service fulfill a need?
- Is my product/service sensitive to economic conditions? If so, what are the factors that affect my business?
- Is my business labor-intensive?
- Do I need in-depth knowledge to operate my business?
- Is my product/service cost sensitive?

- Does my product require creativity, originality, or innovation?
- Does my product/service require ever-changing technology?

Determining the Market

Now that you have defined your business philosophy, you must decide to whom you are going to sell, where they are located, why your product/service is needed, the potential future of the market, what the seasonality for your product/service is, and what percentage share of the market you are aiming for. To assist you in determining your market, the checklist given in Table 16-1 should be completed.

Table 16-1. Checklist for Determining Your Market

Question	Response
In what areas of the country/world do I plan to sell my product or service?	
What is the size of the universe for my product/service?	
What is the growth potential fo my product/service?	
What are the income level, age, and occupation(s) of my customers' universe?	

Table 16-1. Checklist for Determining Your Market (continued)

	Positive	Negative	No Difference	Unknown
What geographical areas offer the greatest potential?				
Who are my major competitors, and what is their estimated share of market?				
What advantages do I enjoy, as compared to my competitors in the following categories? (Check one response.) • Selling price • Quality • Performance • Durability • Practicality • Delivery time • Maintenance • Installation costs • Availability of parts and supplies • Size • Weight • Attractiveness • Other (List below)				

Determining the Method of Distribution

Distribution of your product or service will play a major role in the success or failure of your business. Many business failures are caused by not establishing the most efficient and economical way of getting the product or service to the customer. The form shown in Table 16-2 will be of help in determining the best method of distribution.

Your cost per unit should be compared to that of your competitors. The best method will be the one that gives you the competitive advantage in both cost per unit and servicing of the customer.

Pricing

For pricing strategies, see Chapter 13.

Table 16-2. Method of Distribution Form

Method of Distribution	Cost per Unit	Estimated Competitive per Unit Cost
Your own sales force		
Distributor		
Manufacturer's agent		
Broker		
Wholesaler		
Other (List below.)		

Determining Sales Volume

With your product or service, market, and distribution patterns identified, it is now possible to estimate both unit and dollar sales volume. This forecast should be developed for the length of the business plan. In addition, future sales volume by year should also be projected. The form shown in Table 16-3 can be used for recording this information.

Table 16-3. Form for Recording Sales Volume

| | Product | | | | | | Total | |
| | A | | B | | C | | | |
Period	$	Units	$	Units	$	Units	$	Units
January								
February								
March								
April								
May								
June								
July								
August								
September								
October								
November								
December								
Total								
Year 2								
Year 3								

Determining the Cost of Goods Sold

For each planned unit to be sold, and for each unit that will be needed in inventory in order to service your customers, a unit must be produced. In a manufacturing company, one must consider all of the activities that go into producing a finished product from raw materials. These activities include the acquisition of the raw materials, labor, and overhead needed to support them. Before you can begin to compute the cost of your product, it is necessary to identify the basic steps in the manufacturing of a unit, such as measure and cut, glue and assemble. Use of the form shown in Table 16-4 will facilitate your listing of these activities.

Table 16-4. Form for Listing Activities in Sequence Order

Activities in Sequence Order	Amount of Time to Complete the Activity

Raw Materials

Define how much raw material will be needed and where you intend to buy each item. Be sure you allow enough raw material for waste and for replacement. In addition, certain raw materials may have a short life span in their raw material state and may require brief storage times. It is helpful to record this information on forms, such as those shown in Table 16-5.

Labor

All labor needed to operate the business, including both direct and indirect labor, should be listed on a form such as that shown in Table 16-6.

Table 16-5. Three Forms for Recording Raw Material Use and Cost

Raw Materials Needed	Amount of Materials Needed for Each Unit	Number of Units to be Produced	Total Raw Materials

Raw Materials Needed	Vendor	Price per Unit

Total Raw Materials Needed	Price	Total Raw Material Costs

Table 16-6. Form for Recording Labor Costs

Skills	Required Head Count	Pay Rate	Total Payroll Costs
Direct labor			
Indirect labor			

Overhead

All of the overhead expenses needed to operate the business, including manufacturing and administrative overhead expenses, should be listed on a form such as that shown in Table 16-7.

Determining Facilities and Equipment

The extent of your facilities will depend upon the size of the production facilities and the amount of space needed for both storage and administrative purposes. Cost figures should be developed that take into consideration whether you buy, rent, or lease space; equipment and machinery requirements and the method of acquisition, that is, lease versus buy; and peripheral costs such as parking facilities, warehousing, office space, and office equipment.

Table 16-7. Form for Recording Overhead Expenses

Expense	Monthly Expense	Yearly Expense
Manufacturing overhead Selling overhead Administrative overhead Other (List below.)		

Projecting Profits

Now that most of the input data have been prepared, it is possible to develop a projected statement of all income and expenses for a given period. It is suggested that a month-by-month projection be made for at least one year. Further projections can be made on a yearly basis only. An example of a typical statement is shown in Table 16-8.

Table 16-8. Sample Projected Earnings Statement

	Month 1	Month 2	Month 3
Net sales			
Operating expenses			
Cost of sales			
Materials			
Labor			
Overhead			
Total			
Gross margin			
Other operating expenses			
Depreciation			
Selling expenses			
Advertising expenses			
Administrative expenses			
General expenses			
Operating profit			
Other (income) expense			
Income before income taxes			
Estimated income taxes			
Net earnings			

Projecting Cash Needs

From projected income and expenses an estimated cash forecast should be prepared for the length of the business plan. Monthly projections are recommended. The format shown in Table 16-9 should be used in developing the overall cash forecast. (For further discussion of this subject, see Chapter 3.)

Table 16-9. Form for Showing Estimated Forecast of Cash

	Month 1
Beginning-of-month bank balance	
Cash on hand (petty cash)	
Total cash available at beginning of month	
Estimated accounts receivable collected	
Estimated additional income to be received	
Total estimated monies to be received	
Total cash and monies to be received	
Estimated disbursements	
End-of-month cash balance	

Developing a Balance Sheet

Because a balance sheet reflects the financial condition of your company as of a specific date, it is important that this statement be prepared as of the close of each period. The balance sheet will reflect the assets of the business as well as liabilities to creditors and the owners. (For further analysis of how the balance sheet is prepared, see Chapter 1.)

Other Elements of the Business Plan

Other segments of the business plan need to be developed. They include organization, pricing, financing, creating an image, company policies and procedures, and advertising strategies and will reflect your company's strategy, direction, and philosophy of business operation. These elements should be prepared with the assistance of experts in each functional activity. Many of these elements will change from time to time as the business grows and matures.

Summary

Your business plan must reflect changing conditions as they arise. Your customers will dictate change, the economy will force change, and technology will create change. As this change occurs, business plans must also change in order to reflect these different conditions. Constant review and modification are always necessary to bringing about a business that is prosperous and that continues to grow at a reasonable rate.

17

Financing Your Business

In the previous chapter, we saw how a business plan is developed. Very often, the plan will highlight the need for additional funds. This need can arise as a result of many situations within the business. Some of these situations are as follows:

- With anticipated sales growth, buildups in inventories are necessary.

- Higher sales generally mean higher accounts receivable.

- Excessive buildups in accounts receivable and inventories may arise because of mismanagement of assets (see Chapter 4).

- Opportunities may arise for acquiring inventory, either raw materials or finished products, at discounted prices or for saving on equipment purchases in order to reduce production costs or other operating costs.

- Additional cash may be required as a result of increased business.

- Capital may be needed for expansion of facilities, new products, increased capacity, and so forth.

- Funds may be needed to meet seasonal patterns for both your own needs and the slowness of payment by your customers.

- Sales volume may decline and/or expenses may increase.

- Repayment of current obligations may require immediate additional funds.

- Sufficient earnings have not been retained in the business.

These situations result in a need for additional funds, which is compounded when many of the situations occur at one time.

Determining Your Needs

The preceding situations will create a need for additional financing. To determine your financial needs, you must resolve some basic questions. The answers to these questions will give you the necessary tools with which to develop the most favorable financing package.

First, you must determine why the funds are needed. As was seen previously, funds can be used in many ways, and each use will have a different need and will require a different amount. The business plan (see Chapter 16) will highlight these financing needs and in what periods they will fall.

Second, you must determine what amount of funds is required. Again, the amount will depend upon the individual need and is highlighted in the business plan.

Third, the preparation of a cash flow statement, as contained in the business plan, will indicate how you will repay the money, in addition to contractual requirements, and in what time periods the money can be repaid. Of course, the ability to generate greater returns from these financing needs will greatly speed up the repayment process. This is evident when computing the ROI expected from capital investments.

The last question that must be answered is whether the business can generate enough income to repay the anticipated loan. This means that when projections of income and expenses are prepared, there must be sufficient funds generated over and above all costs, including financing costs and the loan principal.

How to Evaluate the Most Feasible Source of Financing

Because there are many vehicles through which you can finance your business, it is important to determine the most feasible and practical financing requirements. Consideration of the following factors will assist you in this most important evaluation process.

The Cost of Financing

A prime consideration is the impact upon the earnings of the company or the amount that is available to the company. Each capital source will have a different impact. For example, a loan would reduce earnings through higher interest costs. Selling equity may dilute the earnings participation to existing shareholders. Selling assets may decrease operating revenues and increase operating costs.

The Risk Involved

Again, the risk will depend upon the type of financing. The ultimate objective is to expose your company to the lowest possible risk. For example, in equity financing, that is, selling shares in the business, the investor, rather than the company, assumes most of the risk. However, such techniques as trade credit, to be discussed later in the chapter, can affect your relationship with your suppliers or your credit rating. Debt financing assumes risk, since it imposes certain repayment obligations that must be met. Failure to meet these obligations can lead to forfeiture of assets used as collateral or, in extreme cases, bankruptcy.

The Impact of Capital Sources
Upon Other Financing Sources

Certain capital sources will place certain restrictions upon other potential capital sources. For example, certain loan agreements prevent you from using such assets as accounts receivable and inventories as collateral for other borrowings. Using trade credit may limit you in taking advantage of more favorable prices from other suppliers since you will be heavily dependent on a few suppliers.

Dilution of Control

In certain loan arrangements, such as with banks, insurance companies, and other financial institutions, voting rights may be relinquished to some extent and in some cases representation on the board of directors may be required. Even in equity financing, some control may also be relinquished. Caution should be taken not to give up too much control when entering into a financing arrangement.

Evaluating What is Available

A company must evaluate what available sources can be utilized. Not all sources are available to a business. For example, trade credit may be completely exhausted, and internal sources may have already been exhausted to their limit.

It is suggested that all available sources be carefully reviewed to determine what sources are available at what cost and at what risk and the extent of control that must be released. After these factors have been determined, and only then, can important financing decisions be made.

Internal Financing

There are many ways of generating funds internally. These sources may or may not incur additional costs, and in most cases no loss of control is relinquished. The availability of such capital sources is limited, and external funds must be sought to supplement the required capital needed.

Internal Operations

The ability to generate funds through internal operations can sometimes be overlooked. Business managers must look within the company for ways of creating the much-needed capital for keeping the business operating effectively. Let us review some of the ways capital can be generated from internal operations.

Reducing Costs

In any business environment, there are always opportunities for reducing costs. Reductions can be made in the costs of manufacturing and/or of services, labor costs, utilities, administrative costs, purchasing costs, and so forth. Controls should be established to ensure that any costs associated with operating the business are kept to minimum levels. Periodic reviews will also highlight areas where excessive costs occur. However, reducing costs at the expense of losing business must be carefully evaluated. For example, reducing production may leave inventory levels below what is needed to meet your customers' needs. Out-of-stock items may force customers to seek other suppliers.

Managing Your Assets

Assets must be reviewed continuously for excessiveness as well as for being nonproductive. Accounts receivable, inventories, and fixed assets are usually the most obvious. Not having an effective asset management program is one of the major causes of cash shortages in a business. Of course, the management and use of working capital cannot be excluded. (For more detailed discussion of these subjects, see Chapters 4 and 5.)

Retaining Sufficient Earnings in the Business

In many cases, businesses can meet rising capital needs by retaining more of the earnings in the business. This is accomplished by either eliminating or reducing dividend and/or earnings distributions to owners. This retention will be a major source of cash and a major factor in reducing external capital requirements. In addition, lenders will look favorably on a business that generates funds internally before seeking external funds, particularly in meeting debt obligations.

Trade Credit

Credit from suppliers may be extended to provide additional capital in the short term. This short-term approach can be accomplished in many ways. Remember that, in many cases, the relationship with your supplier will determine how effective trade credit can be in generating funds. Some of the ways of using trade credit are as follows:

- The most obvious way of taking advantage of trade credit is to pay invoices on the last possible date. For example, when discounts are available, take the discount on the last available day. In the case of an invoice with terms of 2% net 10 days, the payment would be made on the 10th day. Where no discount is offered, such as net 30 days, make the payment on the 30th day.

- Try to negotiate extended terms from your suppliers. For example, when purchases are received during the month and the terms are net 30 days, negotiating payment terms from the end of the month would give your company some extra days.

- If your relationships with your suppliers are favorable, you may be able to negotiate substantial time extensions in paying certain invoices and, in some cases, all payments. Extensions from 30 to 60 days may be possible if friendly supplier relationships are maintained.

- It is important to weigh the cost effect of trade credit versus other alternative financing, such as short-term bank loans. Foregoing a cash discount in favor of using the money for that specific period must also be weighed. For example, given the terms 2% net 30 days, will forfeiting a 2% discount and using the money for the remaining 20 days for other purposes be more beneficial than borrowing money at prevailing interest rates?

- Utilize promissory notes promising payment at some later date. Such a note may or may not involve interest but in any case would give your supplier more confidence in showing your intent to make payment at the specified date.

Trade credit does have some risk and may not always be available. The risk involves your suppliers, who may refuse to make further shipments in cases where extended trade credit is consistently used. They may feel that your company is unable to meet payments because of the unavailability of cash and may put your company on a cash-on-delivery basis. Some of your suppliers may refuse to extend further trade credit to your company, in which case trade credit is no longer available as a means of raising short-term funds internally. Because trade credit is not always available, it is best to use it wisely for the short term and in small amounts.

Financing from Your Customers

In certain instances, or in certain situations, some advance payment may be required from your customers. This is a form of temporary financing and should be explored as a method of financing internally. For example, deposits, prepayments, progress payments, and supplying raw materials in advance are all types of temporary financing from your customers.

Other

There are other types of financing methods that can be developed. For example, turning equities in buildings and land into cash by mortgaging. In addition, such other techniques as leasing, sale and leaseback agreements and equipment loans are also available.

Debt Financing

Debt financing may take many different forms and may be borrowed for the short term, usually less than one year, or for the long term, more than one year. In any case, *debt financing* is borrowing an amount of money from a creditor. This amount is usually accompanied by a formal document, or note, in which the borrower agrees to repay the borrowed principal plus interest in specified amounts on specified dates. The schedule of payments, the terms of interest, and the length of time are usually negotiated.

Debt financing may not always be available because of lenders' having doubts about the nature of your business; the future of your business in terms of its financial capability, the industry, the product, the markets, and so forth; or, in some cases, the ability of the management to operate the business effectively. In addition, the supply of money may be such that only preferred customers of lending institutions would have access to these funds. For example, when the money market is low, such financial institutions as banks are limited to how much they will lend to their customers and tend to select only borrowers that have had a continuous and profitable relationship with very little risk involved. Other factors such as the financial conditions, stability, and liquidity of the company will also play a major role in whether or not to lend the needed funds to companies.

Debt sources are also available through many different types of financial institutions. Let us review some of these sources and the types of financing that are available.

Bank Financing

Banks, particularly commercial banks, are a major source of funds. They provide short-term loans such as commercial loans, lines of credit, inventory financing, and accounts receivable financing. They also provide both medium- and long-term loans in the form of unsecured term loans, financing of real estate and equipment, and leasing.

The criteria for bank loans will vary from period to period and from borrower to borrower. However, there are generally accepted criteria that banks as well as other lending institutions look for in loan applications. They are the experience of the borrower in both prior loan agreements and business experience; forms of collateral that are available; and the potential ability of the borrower's business to repay the terms of the loan.

Financing through Commercial Finance Companies

When bank loans are denied, or when additional funds are needed over and above other finance sources, a source can be found in commercial finance companies. However, unlike some banks, commercial finance companies usually require some form of collateral such as accounts receivable and inventories. In addition, they also will be involved in equipment leasing and factoring. Because commercial finance companies usually deal in higher risk situations, their rates often are higher than bank rates.

Savings and Loan Companies

This source of funds deals primarily with loans on commercial, industrial, and residential real estate. The ability to repay the debt is usually the most important factor.

Other

Other sources of funds involving debt include life insurance companies, factors, consumer finance companies, small business administration loans, and governmental agencies such as state and local industrial development administrations. Because these sources may not be available to all companies, it is important that you seek some assistance in advance in order to see if you qualify for a particular type of loan agreement.

Equity Financing

The concept of equity capital is different from that of debt financing. Although both are sources of capital, there is no obligation to repay any of the amounts, including interest, under equity financing, which was permanently invested in the business. This permanent investment of capital by investors entitles them to share in some form of earnings distribution and is considered an ownership in the enterprise. This form of ownership may entitle the investor to some voting rights, but not necessarily in operating the business.

In corporate organizations, money can be raised through the selling of equities such as common stock, preferred stock, debentures, and warrants. Each vehicle has a different obligation to its investors, and legal as well as financial assistance should be sought. Keep in mind that public offerings of equity may result in the giving up of some control in the business. However, the equity investor usually assumes most of the risk.

Calculating the Cost of Financing Debt versus Equity

One of the prime considerations in choosing either debt or equity financing, or both, is the ultimate cost incurred in acquiring the funds. A simple illustration will highlight this point.

Calculating the Cost of Debt Financing

Assuming a company wanted to borrow $100,000 at a 15% interest rate with an effective tax rate for the company of 30%, what is the cost of debt financing? Using the following formula, the cost of debt financing is 10.5%, calculated as follows:

Cost of debt financing = Interest rate × (1.00 −
effective income tax rate)

Cost of debt financing = 0.15 × (1.00 − 0.30)
= 0.15 × .70
= 0.105, or 10.5%

Calculating the Cost of Equity Financing

In calculating the cost of equity financing, earnings per
share must be computed. These earnings represent the
amount available for distribution to stockholders or
investors of the company divided by the number of outstanding shares. Of course, consideration must be given
to preferred stockholders and their first priority on the net
earnings of the company.

The cost is computed by dividing anticipated earnings
per share by the selling price of new issue. For example,
if a company is selling its new issue at $16.00 per share,
and the anticipated earnings per share is $2.00, the cost
of this equity financing is 12.5%, as follows:

$$\frac{\$2.00}{\$16.00} = 12.5\%$$

For a more sophisticated method using the average
weighted cost of capital, see Chapter 2.

Comparing Debt and Equity Financing

When comparing debt versus equity financing of your
business, it is important to look at several factors before
making your decision. These factors are the impact upon
the company, the giving up of control, the amount of risk
involved, and the cost (see previous discussion).

Impact upon the Company

In most cases, equity financing will not have a negative
impact upon the flexibility of operating the company.
Debt financing may limit the company's ability to pursue
other opportunities in both financing and growth situations. This may be due to certain restrictions on assets and
other conditions of loan agreements. In addition, higher
debt obligations may discourage other lenders and

creditors from providing future sources of capital to your business.

The Factor of Control

Generally, lenders do not have any voice in operating the business. There are occasions when lenders may require some voice through board of director representation or other ways of approving major decisions. Because equity investors are technically part owners of the business, their control would depend on what percentage of the business they hold in stock or on other agreed-upon bases, as in a partnership. Obviously, the greater the percentage of ownership, the greater the control.

Differences in Risk

As was mentioned previously, equity capital involves very little risk to the company. The investor usually absorbs all the risks and shares in the rewards. When a company prospers, so does the investor. Conversely, when the company does not succeed, neither does the investor, because he or she is looking to return a fair share on the investment through earnings and/or appreciation of the stock. Debt financing involves substantial risk because both principal and interest payments are of an obligatory nature. Default of these payments could lead to serious financial difficulties.

Summary

Choosing the right financing source can help you to avoid many problems in later years. It will also put your company in a more suitable position to obtain further capital and to provide the needed funds to grow. Remember that the ability to choose the right financing is a key element in the success of your business.

Glossary

absorption costing a costing approach whereby both variable and fixed manufacturing costs are charged to all units produced.

acid test ratio supplements the current ratio by measuring liquidity and the ability of the company to meet its current obligations.

accounts payable monies owed creditors for which merchandise was bought on account.

accounts receivable an asset representing monies sold on account and not yet collected.

accounts receivable-net to working capital measures the impact of accounts receivables on liquidity of the company.

accrued expenses a balance sheet account representing monies due but unpaid such as employees salaries and wages, pensions, etc.

adjusted income method a cash budget method that adjusts net earnings to a cash basis by adding or subtracting all transactions that affect or do not affect actual cash.

administrative budget a budget that reflects all the expenses of departments or segments of the business classified as administrative.

analytical reports reports that provide analytical information for interpreting performance of specific segments of the company as well as trends.

assets accounts of the balance sheet representing what a company owns.

assignable costs   costs that are incurred to a specific project.

balance sheet   a financial statement that represents a financial picture of your company at any given point in time. This statement is in balance when assets equal liabilities plus shareholders' equity.

book costs   costs in which accounting allocations of prior expenditures were made to the current period.

bottom-up method   a budgeting method that starts from the lowest operating level and is based on the goals and objectives for each segment of the company.

breakeven point   the breakeven point is reached when net sales equals variable costs plus fixed costs.

budget   represents a formal expression of the plans and objectives of management's ideas and expectations covering all activities of the company's operation for a specific period of time.

budgeting   refers to all of the processes of preparing a budget, the coordination, the control, the reporting of variances, and all the policies and procedures needed to accomplish a company's objective.

budgeting process   brings together all of the planned activities of a company into a meaningful set of actions.

calendar year   financial results of a 12 month period for a year beginning January 1st and ending December 31st.

capital stock   represents the shares the owners have in the interest of the company.

capital surplus   represents an amount paid in by the shareholders over and above the par or legal value of each share of stock.

cash flow   for computing projections for capital investment proposals, accounting net earnings plus depreciation charges are used.

cash in banks   an asset representing money on hand or held in banking accounts.

cash receipts and disbursements method   a cash budget that forecasts cash by tracing thru all the items of income and expense.

compounding   a method used to compute a sum of money at the present time to another sum of money at the end of X years.

contribution margin   concept of breakeven that solves how many units are necessary to recover both fixed costs and yet generate a desired profit.

contribution pricing   a pricing approach where the best price is the one that generates the highest contribution.

cost centers   a segment of the business that incurs cost, but does not generate revenues.

cost of capital   average rate of earnings which investor's require to induce them to provide all forms of long-term capital to the company.

cost of sales   costs of manufacturing a product such as materials, labor and overhead.

cost of sales to inventories   measures the turnover of inventory.

cost reduction projects   projects that result in the reduction of costs.

current assets   assets used in the normal course of business which can be converted into cash more quickly than other assets.

current liabilities   debts of a company that fall due within the current calendar or fiscal year.

current liabilities to shareholders' equity   measures the share creditors have against the company as compared to the shareholders'.

current ratio   measures the ability of the company to meet its current obligations.

day's sales on hand   indicates the average length in days that inventory is held before it is sold.

day's sales outstanding   ratio referred to as the collection period and indicates the average age of net customer's accounts receivable.

debt due after one-year   monies owed lenders beyond one year of the date of the balance sheet.

debt due within one-year   monies due lenders and payable within the current calendar or fiscal year.

debt to equity   measures the amount a company is financed by long-term debt or borrowed capital, and the extent to which a company is financed by permanent contributed capital.

depreciation periodic write-offs of expenses to account for the wear and tear of a physical asset such as buildings, machinery and equipment.

direct costing a costing approach that only allocates variable costs to the product.

direct labor amount of labor needed to convert materials used into a finished product.

direct labor budget determines the amount of personnel needed both in headcount and dollars to fulfill the requirements of the production budget.

direct materials represents materials that are used to manufacture a product and ultimately becomes part of a product produced.

discounted cash flow the basic theory of DCF says that a dollar today is worth more than a dollar in the future.

discounting a method that shifts the value of money to be received in the future back to the present.

earnings retained in business the amount accumulated and left in the business after payment of dividends to shareholders.

earnings statement a financial statement that reflects how much profit was made during a given period by recording all transactions of income and expenses.

expansion capacity projects projects whose primary purpose is to increase production.

financial budgets budget activity that relates to the balance sheet and the company's financial condition as of a specified period.

fiscal year financial results of a 12 month period other than January 1st to December 31st.

fixed assets assets that are not intended for sale, but are used in either the manufacturing, distributing, warehousing, shipping or selling of the product.

fixed costs costs that do not fluctuate as levels of activity vary.

forecast a projection of activity for a specified period of time.

gross margin percent indicates the margin of sales over the cost of sales.

high price strategy   pricing technique whereby higher than usual prices are established on selected products.

human resources budget   reflects the human resource requirements of the company.

in and out pricing   a pricing strategy that prices products high and price reductions occur when the segment of the market sought after becomes saturated.

incremental cost method   a mark-up method of pricing that emphasizes the conversion costs, and shifts the emphasis on products that have high material costs.

internal rate of return method   this method solves for the discount or interest rate that discounts cash flow to equal the investment.

inventories   an asset representing merchandise in the form of either raw materials, in-process merchandise, or finished goods.

inventories to working capital   measures the impact of inventories on the liquidity of the company.

investment centers   a unit of an organization whereby investment dollars are controlled and is measured by the amount of earnings generated from a specific amount of investment.

job costing   cost system method that accumulates costs of an identifiable product known as a job, and follows the product through the production stages.

liabilities   accounts of the balance sheet representing what a company owes to both creditors and shareholders.

manufacturing overhead   manufacturing costs of producing a product over and above direct materials and direct labor.

managing ratios   ratios that assist in evaluating the various components of the balance sheet.

margin of safety   calculation of breakeven that reflects how much sales can decrease before losses can be expected.

margin rate   result of the selling price less variable costs.

marketable securities   an asset representing temporary investments in securities of excess cash and held for short periods of time.

net earnings   result of net sales less all operating expenses, net of other income (expense) and income taxes.

net earnings to net sales   measures the profitability of every dollar of sales. Also referred to as the profitability rate.

net earnings to shareholders' equity   measures the return that is generated from the owners' equity in the business when considering all risks.

net earnings to total assets   represents the return on funds invested in the company by both owners and creditors.

net earnings to working capital   measures the ability of a company to use working capital to generate net earnings.

net present value method   method that calculates the net present value of cash flows using a given discount rate.

net sales   revenues received from customers for the exchange of goods sold or services rendered, and is the prime source of revenues for a company.

net sales to accounts receivable-net   measures the turnover of receivables.

net sales to fixed assets-net   measures how efficient a business is able to use its investments in fixed assets.

net sales to shareholders' equity   measures the amount of sales volume that is supported by the equity of the company.

net sales to working capital   measures the ability of working capital to support levels of sales volume.

new product introduction projects   projects whose primary objective is providing facilities for the introduction of new products.

operating budgets   an estimate of activity whereby both income and expenses are involved and is closely associated with the elements of the earnings statement.

operating expenses   expenses associated with the running of the business in support of selling a product.

operating profit   result of subtracting cost of sales and other operating expenses from net sales.

operational reports   reports that are used in the controlling of the business by highlighting those areas of the company that may need corrective action.

opportunity costs   represents a benefit that is foregone as a result of not using another alternative.

out-of-pocket costs   cost that require cash outlays either currently or in the future.

payback method   calculated by dividing total investment dollars of a capital investment proposal by the annual cash flows.

performance ratios   ratios that follow the trend of the overall performance of the company.

period costs   costs that incurred as a function of time as opposed to levels of activity.

planning reports   reports that deal with anticipated activities at some future date.

prepaid expense   an asset representing prepayments such as insurance premiums.

process costing   cost system method that accumulates costs by a process or operation as it flows through production.

product costs   production costs that relate with the products unit output and charged to the products cost when the product is sold.

profitability rate   measures how much earnings are generated from each dollar of sales.

profitability ratios   ratios that evaluate components of the earnings statement and effectively show how well a manager is performing given the level of responsibility.

profit centers   a business unit which has the responsibility for generating income and responsibility for cost expenditures.

profit contribution ratio   computed by dividing the contribution margin by net sales and is the reciprocal of the relationship of variable costs to net sales.

programmed costs   costs that result from specific decisions without any consideration as to volume activity or passage of time.

psychological pricing   a pricing strategy that prices just below the next dollar amount.

replacement and maintenance projects   projects that are essential to maintaining the current status of the business.

return on investment   a management tool that measures both past performance and future investment decisions in a reasonably systematic manner.

return on investment pricing   a pricing approach which determines the price needed to achieve a desired return on investment.

revenue centers   centers where performance is measured in terms of sales revenues.

sales budget   a budget which develops a forecast of how many new orders and shipments will be made during the budget year.

selling expenses to net sales   measures the cost of selling a product.

shareholders' equity   a liability account that represents the amount of equity interest that shareholders' have in the company.

source and application of funds   indicates how money flows through a business by highlighting where the cash was used and where the cash was spent.

standard costs   anticipated or predetermined costs of producing a unit of output under given conditions.

top-down method   a budgeting method that utilizes a central staff which reflects and determines the corporate goals.

total cost method   a mark-up method of pricing that recoups all costs of the product and adds a desired profit margin to arrive at a selling price.

turnover rate   indicator of how capital intensive a business is, or how many dollars in investment is needed to support dollars in revenues.

typical pricing   a pricing strategy that is generally established by the marketplace.

unassignable costs   costs that cannot be directly traced to a specific product and/or segment of the business without arbitrarily allocating the cost.

variable costs   costs that change in direct proportion to levels of activity.

volume strategy   pricing strategy that accepts low margins, but profits are generated from high volume.

weighted average cost of capital   measures all components of capital and assigns given values for each capital component in accordance with contractual and calculated rates and develops a weighted average cost.

working capital   computed by subtracting current liabilities from current assets.

INDEX